Cassell C...
French

CW00461138

Cassell Guide to French Officialese

Sheelagh Johnson

CASSELL

London and Washington

Cassell
Wellington House, 125 Strand, London WC2R 0BB
PO Box 605, Herndon, VA 20172

First published 1997

The author and publishers wish to thank La Caisse
Nationale de l'Assurance Maladie de la Sécurité Sociale
and Postes and Téléphones for permission to reproduce the
forms on pages 183–196.

British Library Cataloguing-in-Publication Data
A catalogue record for this book is available from the British
Library.

ISBN 0-304-33815-X

Typeset by BookEns Ltd, Royston, Herts
Printed and bound in Great Britain by
Biddles Ltd, Guildford and King's Lynn

Contents

Disclaimer

The author has taken every care in compiling this guide. However, it should **not** be used as a substitute for professional legal advice. The French bureaucratic system is notoriously complex, and its laws and regulations are constantly changing. Even at the best of times, French terms do not always mean what they suggest at first sight, or what their nearest English equivalent or translation means.

It should always be remembered that neither the French language nor its administrative system is a mirror image of its British counterpart. One shared concept may stand for two entirely different realities. Only someone qualified in *French* law should be relied upon for expert advice.

In particular, it is inadvisable to sign or accept any document translated into English that you might one day have to wave in front of a court or other official body in France. As any given English term may be translatable by up to half a dozen French words, you will never be able to prove that what you were promised in English is what you were promised in French.

For this reason, the author and publisher can take no responsibility for the consequences of any action taken or not taken as a result of reading this book.

Notes for the Reader

List of abbreviations

(adj) adjective
(adv) adverb
(n) noun
(nf) feminine noun
(nm) masculine noun
(nm/f) noun that can be either masculine or feminine
(n.pl) noun found in the plural
(pl) plural
(prep) preposition
(qn) quelqu'un (someone)
(qch) quelquechose (something)
(sing) singular
(vb) verb
(vb.int) intransitive verb

Bold lettering

French words are all given in bold, even if they appear within a definition given in English.

Definitions

The definitions of terms given are not exhaustive, but cover only that range of meanings which relate to official documents and procedures. For a fuller account, a conventional dictionary should be consulted.

Definitions are listed in two ways. Commas are used to separate groups of synonyms and related meanings, while brackets containing numbers indicate major differences of usage. For example:

abonné (*nm/f, adj*) a subscriber, contract holder, someone who has taken out an **abonnement**

brevet (*nm*) (1) a licence (pilot's, etc.) (2) a patent (3) a diploma, certificate (4) the series of exams, more formally known as the **brevet des collèges**, taken at the end of the fourth year at school and equivalent to GCSE.

False friends

False friends are words which look similar in French and English, but which have different meanings. Where these are liable to lead to important misunderstandings, the term has been written into the text:

éventuel (*adj*) possible. **éventuellement** (*adv*) possibly. Used often to convey 'perhaps'. A false friend. English *eventually* implies certainty, while the French **éventuelle- ment** implies the opposite. **L'acquéreur éventuel** refers to a *potential* or *possible* buyer, not to 'the person who will eventually but definitely buy it'. A job offer that proposes **une période d'essai qui débouchera éventuellement en un poste permanent** means not 'a trial period that will lead *eventually* to a permanent post', but 'a trial period that *might, perhaps* lead' to one. *See* **dol**, **publicité mensongère**

This is an important distinction for someone trying to decide whether to accept a job offer that will involve abandoning a home and career in Britain in order to emigrate to France.

List of Entries by Subject and Index of English Words

The book is in three parts, firstly the main body of the dictionary, then a list of entries by subject, followed by an index of English words. In the List of Entries, all the terms connected with major topics like the law or employment are listed together in groups. This is to facilitate systematic study of a chosen field, as well as to make the text readable in its own right for those who prefer to browse.

Also at the back of the book is an index of English terms. However, it should be remembered that this is an index, *not* a list of *translations*, though often the direct translation will be listed among the words given. The purpose of the Index is to give access to the French, by listing those entries in French which deal with the topic given in English. For example, under the English term *divorce* are listed '**aliments, conseiller matrimonial, divorce, droit de visite, juge des affaires matrimoniales.** *See* marriage'. The translation is given by the word **divorce**; the other terms refer to issues connected with divorce.

Signposting

To facilitate reading round a subject, at the end of most entries is a list of additional terms related to the main heading. This section is introduced by the word *See*. Where there is a large number of entries on a given topic, the full list is given in one entry only, to which all others are then referred. For example, under **allocation** will be found all the terms relating to financial help, benefits and grants of various kinds: **aide, assistance, avantages, bourse, congé, frais, indemnité, pension, prestation, prime, programme à loyer réduit, quotient familial, revenu minimum d'insertion, subvention, tribunal adminis-tratif.**

Variations in usage

Some official terms are subject to variation or replacement by synonyms, especially when used in compounds. Where one person uses the word **aide** another may use **allocation**. Similarly, where some officials refer to **livret de famille**, others say **bulletin** or **cahier de famille**. Limitations on space prevent all these permutations from being listed, and the terms given are those which are most common in my experience. If a compound term like **aide de logement** is not listed under the principal term, **aide**, the reader should look under the list of related terms, which in this case would include **allocation**.

To Mary, Ray and Kate,
with love

Introduction

This dictionary arose out of personal experience of ten years of living and working in France. It gathers together a wide range of official terms and expressions that can crop up in everyday life in areas like employment, house-buying, renting flats, social services, education, doctors, hospitals, family life, the courts, police, travel, business, industrial tribunals, stocks, shares and local government. Books exist which contain most of the information presented here, but they are expensive, bulky and too numerous to be carried around. Here, for the first time, the information needed to deal with everyday problems is gathered together in a single, cheap, user-friendly volume that will fit easily into the pocket.

The dictionary is not written for specialists. It does not attempt to cover its subject matter exhaustively or systematically. Rather, it opts for those areas which ordinary people are most likely to encounter and have trouble with. For this reason, the book tries where possible to *explain* terms, not simply to translate them. A translation is little use if the word makes no more sense *after* translation than it did before. Officialese knows no boundaries, and French jargon translated into English jargon may be simply the replacement of one foreign language by another. Though most adults have an understanding of basic official terms, whether they can understand a document packed with them is another matter, especially if they have to read it in a hurry. The situation for students of French is similar. Being mostly young, they have not passed through the adult rites of passage like buying a house, signing an employment contract or receiving their first solicitor's letter.

The first aim of the book, therefore, is to allow anglophones to read and fill in French official forms and documents, without having to seek expensive legal or specialist advice. The second aim follows from the first, and is to make it easier for them to understand the French social system and so respect its protocols and, where necessary, to understand what their rights are and how to claim them. Linked to this is the added aim of helping anglophones to avoid pitfalls, for example, when looking for jobs.

A book such as this is more necessary than it might seem at first sight, because, contrary to the popular myth and holiday image of a happy-go-lucky Latin race, the French are an extremely well-ordered, efficient, even bureaucratic people, who set a high value on precision, correct procedure and a suitable official form for every occasion. Worse, the French always seem to have their own way of doing things, and that way is invariably different from the way the rest of the world or common sense would do it. The fact that these idiosyncratic methods have the annoying habit of confounding expectations and working exceptionally well merely adds to the exasperation. To the uninitiated, this can be highly disconcerting, especially if they have just emigrated, and are confronted by not one, but a seemingly endless procession of such formalities. It is for such people, in particular, that the dictionary is designed.

But the book also has another, wider aim, which is to serve as a cultural introduction to France and the Gallic mentality. The book is more than a glossary alone. Entries are signposted, so that the text can be read in its own right, not solely as a reference work. Readers can work their way around a subject like house-buying or employment law, either for systematic study or for the pleasure of browsing. I hope the book will interest not only anglophones with a professional interest in France, but anyone with a concern for French culture and cultural difference in general.

Sheelagh Johnson
University of Lincolnshire and Humberside

A

à percevoir (*adj*) reverse-charge (telephone call), available now only for international dialling

à pourvoir (*adj*) **un poste à pourvoir** a post that is vacant, a post to be filled

à restaurer *see* **restaurer**

abonné (*nm/f, adj*) a subscriber, contract holder, someone who has taken out an **abonnement**

abonnement (*nm*) (1) a subscription (to a magazine, etc.) (2) a season ticket (3) a rental agreement (for a TV, etc.)

abusif/ive (*adj*) improper, unfair. *See* **licenciement**

accise (*nf*) excise duty. *See* **tarif, taxe**

accord collectif (*nm*) *same as* **convention collective**

accroissement temporaire d'activité (*nm*) temporary increase in business activity. *See* **contrat de travail à durée déterminée, motif de l'appel, travail temporaire**

accusation (*nf*) (1) an accusation (2) an indictment, charge. **abandonner l'accusation** to drop the charges. **mise en accusation** indictment

accusé/e (*nm/f*) (1) the accused, defendant (2) **accusé de réception** an acknowledgement of receipt (for a recorded letter). *See* **assigné, défendeur, inculpé, justiciable, prévenu, responsable**

accuser réception (*vb*) to acknowledge receipt of (**de**). *See* **lettre recommandée**

achat à crédit (*nm*) *see* **crédit**

acompte (*nm*) a down payment, payment on account, (financial) advance

acquéreur (*nm*) a buyer, purchaser. *See* **assurance automatique acquéreur**

1

acte (*nm*) a written document. *See* **avis**, **exploit**

acte authentique (*nm*) a contract drawn up by a solicitor (**notaire**) on a special form (**papier timbré**) on which stamp duty has been paid, then signed by the solicitor and both parties involved. This type of document has great legal force, and is presumed in law to be valid unless it can be proved otherwise. Many agreements – such as one to buy a house – are carried out in this form, rather than simply by being signed in the presence of a witness (a contract known as an **acte sous-seing privé**). The **acte authentique** is also known as an **acte notarié**. *See* **testament**

acte d'achat (*nm*) *see* **acte de vente**

acte d'acquisition (*nm*) a deed of purchase, bill of sale (for a building plot, etc.). *See* **acte de vente**

acte d'association (*nm*) a partnership agreement, a contract legally confirming a partnership

acte de baptême (*nm*) a baptism certificate

acte de décès (*nm*) a death certificate. *See* **déclaration de non-décès**

acte de l'état civil (*nm*) a document giving details of an aspect of a person's official status in society, such as a birth, marriage or death certificate. *See* **état civil**, **livret de famille**

acte de mariage (*nm*) a marriage certificate. *See* **communauté**, **dispense de bans**, **extrait**, **livret de famille**

acte de notoriété (*nm*) a certificate issued in an emergency by a judge of the **tribunal d'instance** confirming details of a missing official document, such as a birth or marriage certificate. *See* **ampliation**, **état civil**, **livret de famille**, **notoriété**

acte de succession (*nm*) a certificate or attestation of inheritance. *See* **succession**

acte de vente (*nm*) a bill of sale, a conveyance, a deed confirming the sale of property or land. Though both a buyer and a seller are involved, and the term **acte d'achat**

(bill of purchase) also exists, **acte de vente** is normally used by both parties. *See* **contrat de réservation, promesse de vente**

acte notarié (*nm*) *same as* **acte authentique**

acte solennel (*nm*) a legally certified document or deed. *See* **acte authentique, timbre**

acte sous-seing privé (*nm*) a private agreement; a privately signed contract, which is not legally certified, and must be proved authentic should dispute arise. A less formal alternative to an **acte authentique** and common in house-buying

acte sur papier timbré (*nm*) a legally certified, official document bearing a stamp. *See* **acte authentique, timbre**

actifs (*nm.pl*) (1) a workforce, employees (in a particular business) (2) a working population (3) assets. **porter une somme à l'actif** to include a sum of money on the assets side

action (*nf*) (1) a lawsuit. **intenter une action contre** to bring an action against someone

action civile (*nf*) a civil action, civil case

action en diffamation (*nf*) a libel action. *See* **dénonciation calomnieuse**

action en justice (*nf*) a legal action, lawsuit, court case. *See* **affaire, contentieux, saisir la justice**

action juridique (*nf*) a legal action

action publique (*nf*) a lawsuit or proceedings brought against someone by the authorities

action (*nf*) (2) a share (registered). **actions** (*nf.pl*) stocks, shares

action au porteur (*nf*) a bearer share

action libérée (*nf*) a fully paid-up share

action ordinaire (*nf*) an ordinary share

action privilégiée (*nf*) a preference share

action sanitaire et sociale (nf) see **Direction Départementale de l'Action Sanitaire et Sociale** or **DDASS** (pronounced dass)

actionnaire (nm/f) a shareholder

actionner (vb) to sue, take legal action against. See **action**

adjudication (nf) (1) an invitation to tender   (2) the awarding (of a contract)

administrateur/trice (nm/f) (1) a director   (2) a trustee   (3) an administrator (of a will). See **exécuteur, testament**

administrateur judiciaire (nm) a receiver

administratif/ive (adj) administrative. See **cité**

administration (nf) administration, management, government, running. **l'Administration** the Civil Service, the government services

Administration des Douanes (nf) Customs and Excise. See **accise, franchise, police de l'air et des frontières**

Administration des Eaux et Forêts (nf) the Forestry Commission

Administration des Impôts (nf) the tax department, Inland Revenue. See **fisc, percepteur**

administration locale (nf) local government. See **accise, arrêté**

administrativement (adv) officially, as a result of an official decision

administré/e (nm/f) a term for any individual who is subject to the rule of the French Administration. Every French citizen is an **administré**.

adversaire (nm/f) an opponent in a court case. Sometimes referred to as the **partie adversaire**

affaire (nf) (1) business (in the sense of matter, problem)   (2) business (in the sense of a commercial enterprise). See **affaires**   (3) a case (in law or police work). **porter une affaire devant un tribunal** to take a case to court

affaire-test (*nf*) a test case. *More fully* **affaire-test destinée à faire jurisprudence** a test case aimed at changing the law

affaires (*nf.pl*) business (in general). **homme d'affaires** a businessman

affectation (*nf*) allocation, allotment (of money, a flat, etc.)

agence (*nf*) an agency, office, bureau, branch. *See* **agent**

> **agence commerciale** (*nf*) the sales department or sales outlet of a business. *See* **agent commercial**
>
> **agence comptable** (*nf*) (1) an accountant, in the sense of the office in which he or she works   (2) a firm of accountants. *See* **agence fiscale accréditée**
>
> **agence d'assurance** (*nf*) an insurance agency. *See* **assurance**
>
> **agence de placement** (*nf*) an employment agency
>
> **agence de publicité** (*nf*) an advertising agency, publicity agency
>
> **agence de renseignements** (*nf*) an information bureau
>
> **agence de travail** (*nf*) *see* **travail temporaire**
>
> **agence fiscale accréditée** (*nf*) an accountant's office dealing with private financial and tax problems. *See* **agence comptable, plus-value**
>
> **agence immobilière** (*nf*) an estate agent's office
>
> **agence maritime** (*nf*) a shipping agent
>
> **agence matrimoniale** (*nf*) a marriage bureau. *See* **communauté, mariage**
>
> **Agence Nationale pour l'Amélioration de l'Habitat (ANAH)** (*nf*) a State body giving grants for home improvements. These cover insulation and energy-saving in the case of houses built before 1975, and general building and sanitation in the case of those constructed before 1948.
>
> **Agence Nationale pour l'Amélioration des Conditions d'Emploi** (*nf*) a State body concerned with the monitoring of conditions in the workplace. *See* **Inspection du Travail**

Agence Nationale pour l'Emploi (ANPE) (*nf*) (1) a job centre   (2) the government department that runs the job centres. *See* **agence de placement, travail temporaire**

agent (*nm*) an agent, officer, particularly someone who works for the State or in an **agence**

agent commercial (*nm*) a sales rep, salesman

agent comptable (*nm*) an accountant. *See* **comptabilité**

agent d'affaires (*nm*) a businessman, businesswoman

agent de fisc (*nm*) a tax inspector. *See* **impôt, perception, taxe**

agent de police (*nm*) a policeman. *See* **commissariat, police**

agent titulaire (*nm*) a civil servant with security of tenure for life. *See* **auxiliaire, fonctionnaire, titulaire**

agent voyer (*nm*) a borough surveyor. *See* **géomètre-expert**

agglomération (*nf*) (1) a conurbation. **l'agglomération tolosane** the greater Toulouse area   (2) a federation (of **communes**)

AGIRC *see* **Association Générale des Institutions de Retraite des Cadres**

agréé par l'Etat (*adj*) government-approved

agrégation (*nf*) the most prestigious of the competitive exams for secondary teachers, granting the recipient the title of **professeur agrégé**. *See* **certificat, concours, école, équivalence, lycée**

aide (*nf*) aid, assistance, a grant. *See below and* **allocation, facultatif**

aide au retour (*nf*) a repatriation grant; payment to help immigrants (from non-EU countries) to leave France and return to their homeland

aide facultative (*nf*) discretionary aid or assistance. Money which is only paid out if the people claiming it can convince the official responsible that they are a special case. *See* **aide légale**

aide financière (*nf*) financial aid, help with payment of something. *See* **allocation, avantages, prestation**

aide judiciaire (*nf*) legal aid, financial help with legal fees in a court case. *See* **aide légale**

aide légale (*nf*) mandatory or statutory aid. Awards, grants or payments to which the claimant has an automatic, legal right. The opposite of a discretionary award (**aide facultative**), which is one paid or not paid according to the merits of each individual case. Not to be confused with legal aid, in the sense of financial help given to people bringing court cases, which is **aide judiciaire**

aide médicale (*nf*) help with medical fees

aide ménagère (*nf*) home help for old or disabled people, for up to sixty hours per month. The service is normally run locally by the **centre communal d'action sociale**. *See* **allocation, obligation alimentaire, recouvrement par succession**

aide personnalisée au logement (APL) (*nf*) payments made by the State to help with home-buying, home improvements or rent, for people on low incomes. The payment is made directly to the landlord or loan company. This service is in the process of being phased out. *See* **Agence Nationale pour l'Amélioration de l'Habitat, allocation logement, programme à loyer réduit**

aide sociale (*nf*) welfare, social security. A form of supplementary benefit paid to those who do not qualify for regular unemployment pay. *See* **Bureau Aide Sociale**

aide (*nm/f*) an assistant, helper, (workman's) mate. **aide-électricien** an electrician's mate. **aide familiale** a home help. *See* **allocation de garde de famille à domicile**

ajournement (*nm*) (1) adjournment, postponement, deferment, putting back (of a meeting, etc.) (2) a summons. *See* **exploit d'ajournement, renvoyer, reporter**

ajourner (*vb*) (1) to adjourn, postpone, put back (2) to summon to appear (before a court, etc.). **exploit d'ajournement** a writ or summons to appear

alcool au volant (nm) drink-driving

alcootest/alcooltest (nm) the breathalyser test. The amount of alcohol permitted in drivers' blood is comparable to that in the UK, but the penalties for failing the test are more severe, including imprisonment and automatic disqualification. The test can be imposed at random on drivers. See **casier**

alimentaire (adj) see **obligation alimentaire**

aliments (nm.pl) maintenance payments (in divorce cases, etc.)

alinéa (nm) a sub-paragraph, usually in an official document. See **avenant**

allégation (nf) an allegation

aller en justice (vb) to take a case to court, to take legal action. See **actionner, affaire, ester en justice, poursuivre en justice**

Alliance Française (nf) an organization, on the lines of the British Council, which promotes French culture abroad. London, like most major cities, has an **Alliance Française**, offering courses on French language, history and culture.

allocation (nf) an allowance, grant, usually in the sense of one paid by the **Sécurité Sociale**. See below and **aide, assistance, avantages, bourse, congé, frais, indemnité, pension, prestation, prime, programme à loyer réduit, quotient familial, revenu minimum d'insertion, subvention, tribunal administratif**

allocation assistante maternelle (nf) child-minder's fees, paid for children under the age of 3, to parents who have taken out a special Social Security scheme

allocation aux adultes handicapés (nf) invalidity benefit paid to those unable to find work because of disability

allocation aux mères de famille (nf) a special pension paid to retired mothers of large families, who would not otherwise be entitled to state benefits. See **famille nombreuse**

allocation compensatrice de handicap (nf) an allowance paid to disabled people either for home help or for work expenses

allocation de base (*nf*) the basic rate of unemployment benefit

allocation de chômage (*nf*) the dole, unemployment pay. There are a number of forms of this, some listed below.

allocation d'éducation spécialisée/spéciale (*nf*) an allowance paid to the parents of children up to the age of 20 who have special educational needs

allocation de fin de droit (*nf*) unemployment benefits paid to people who have exhausted their right to regular unemployment pay (**allocation de base**)

allocation de garde de famille à domicile (*nf*) home help allowance for child care, in households where both parents are out at work. *See* **allocation pour frais de garde**

allocation d'insertion (*nf*) benefits paid to people not entitled to regular state benefits, such as young people, refugees, etc.

allocation de loyer (*nf*) rent allowance (for old people and those on low incomes, etc.). *See* **aide personnalisée au logement, allocation logement, avantages en nature nourriture et logement, programme à loyer réduit**

allocation de parent isolé (*nf*) an allowance paid to single mothers or pregnant women, whether unmarried or separated. *See below*

allocation de rentrée scolaire (*nf*) an allowance paid in September to parents of children returning to school, who qualify for certain other benefits. *See* **rentrée**

allocation de salaire unique (*nf*) an allowance paid to families with a single income. *See above*

allocation de solidarité (*nf*) benefits paid to unemployed people who have exhausted their entitlement to **allocation de fin de droit**

allocation de soutien familial (*nf*) a single parent's allowance, which tops up the **allocation familiale** when an absent partner fails to provide maintenance. It is paid by the **caisse d'allocations familiales**, which then attempts to recover the amount from the absent partner. *See* **pension alimentaire**

allocation des mineurs handicapés (*nf*) a handicapped child's allowance

allocation familiale (*nf*) child benefit paid to the parent of two or more children under the age of 20

allocation logement (*nf*) an additional housing benefit paid to people with special needs, including young married couples. *See* **allocation de loyer**

allocation militaire (*nf*) an allowance paid to the dependants of those on national service

allocation post-natale (*nf*) newborn baby's allowance, paid to the mothers of very young children. *See* **allocation pour jeune enfant**

allocation pour frais de garde (*nf*) financial help with child-minding fees. *See* **allocation de garde de famille à domicile**

allocation pour jeune enfant (*nf*) infant's allowance paid by the State. This is split into two parts, **allocation prénatale**, paid to all women for nine months from the fourth month of pregnancy, and **allocation post-natale**, a means-tested benefit paid from then on if the child survives, until the third birthday. Both allowances require the mother to agree to medical and other check-ups. *See also* **congé de maternité, frais d'accouchement**

allocation prénatale (*nf*) a new mother's allowance. *See* **allocation pour jeune enfant**

allocation spéciale (vieillesse) (*nf*) an allowance paid by the local authority to retired people who have no state pension or only limited means

allocation spéciale mi-temps (*nf*) an allowance paid by the State to encourage the creation of part-time jobs which otherwise would not be financially viable. *See* **Fonds National de l'Emploi**

allocation supplémentaire du fonds national de solidarité (*nf*) an allowance paid to old or disabled people who have difficulty looking after themselves, which helps pay for home help or sheltered accommodation. *See above and* **allocation de loyer, allocation logement, centre communal d'action sociale, obligation alimentaire**

amélioration des conditions du travail (*nf*) *see* **Agence Nationale pour l'Amélioration des Conditions d'Emploi**

amende (*nf*) a fine, penalty. **amende forfaitaire** a fixed-penalty fine, which can be paid without the need for a court appearance. If not paid within thirty days, the amount payable is automatically increased (**majoré**).

amiable (*adj*) amicable, informal, private, out-of-court (in a legal sense). **liquider une affaire à l'amiable** to settle out of court. **accord à l'amiable** a friendly or amicable agreement. **vente à l'amiable** a private sale. *See* **constat amiable, particulier**

amiable compositeur (*nm*) a go-between, independent arbitrator. Someone who mediates informally between the parties in a dispute, usually in an attempt to avoid the matter having to go to court. *See* **arbitrage, conciliation, liquider une affaire à l'amiable** (*above*)

amnistie (*nf*) an amnesty, usually in the sense of an amnesty law (*loi d'amnistie*). These usually follow a presidential election, when it has been customary for the **Assemblée Nationale** to pass a bill to grant an amnesty for certain kinds of less serious offence, ranging from motoring fines to prison sentences.

amnistie fiscale (*nf*) an amnesty of the above type, but issued by the tax authorities, in the hope of getting tax-dodgers of various kinds to come forward

ampliation (*nf*) a certified copy of an official document. *See* **acte de notoriété, expédition, levée de jugement**

amplitude journalière (*nf*) the length of time during a day in which the employee is available *for* work, or **disponible au travail**. This is not to be confused with the length of time the employee is *at* work and for which pay is received, or **durée quotidienne du travail**. It represents the period of time between *arriving* at work and *leaving* work, but not the time spent in paid work. An employee, especially a foreign one, may be *compelled* to be available at the place of work for far longer than he or she is actually working.

ANAH *see* **Agence Nationale pour l'Amélioration de l'Habitat**

ancienneté (*nf*) (1) length of service in a post   (2) seniority. **cinq ans d'ancienneté** five years' service. **à l'ancienneté** according to seniority

ANIL a national association for information on buildings. An advisory body with an office in most **départements** which gives information and advice to prospective property buyers, tenants or house-builders

année civile (*nf*) a calendar year

année fiscale (*nf*) a financial year, fiscal year, tax year

année scolaire (*nf*) the school year, which runs from early September to early June. *See* **école, rentrée, scolarisation**

annexe (*nf*) an annexe to or supplement to a document. *See* **avenant**

annexe (*adj*) attached, annexed, added, appended (of pages to a letter, etc.). *See* **ci-joint**

ANPE (**Agence Nationale pour l'Emploi**) the job centre, national employment agency. This has a reputation for not being particularly helpful to foreigners looking for jobs. *See* **agence de placement, travail**

ANTIOPE teletext. The letters stand for **Acquisition Numérique et Télévisualisation d'Images Organisées en Pages d'Ecriture**

APEC *see* **Association pour l'Emploi des Cadres**

APL *see* **aide personnalisée au logement**

appel (*nm*) an appeal (against a court or official judgement). Almost 50 per cent of French court judgements are appealed against. *See* **contradictoire, cour d'appel, cour de cassation, instance**

appelant/e (*nm/f*) an appellant, the person who brings or makes an appeal (to a court or other official body)

appelé (*nm*) a conscript, someone who has been called up for national service. *See* **service national**

appeler (*vb*) to call   **appeler les causes** to read out formally the list of cases to be heard (in a court)

apprentissage (*nm*) apprenticeship. *See* **centre de formation d'apprentis**

apurement (*nm*) auditing

AR *see* **avis de réception**

arbitrage (*nm*) arbitration, conciliation, the settling of disputes without recourse to the courts. **maison d'arbitrage** (*nf*) office of the conciliation service. **service d'arbitrage** the conciliation service. *See* **amiable, conciliation, médiation**

ARRCO *see* **Association des Régimes de Retraites Complémentaires**

arrêt (*nm*) (1) a decision or ruling made by the **Conseil d'Etat** or by the court of appeal (**cour d'appel**) (2) a ruling having the force of law (sometimes called **un arrêt de règlement**) (3) a legal attachment, an order authorizing the confiscation of property, goods or belongings in order to pay off a debt. **faire arrêt sur qn** to issue a writ of attachment on somebody. *See* **astreinte**

arrêt de travail (*nm*) (1) a stoppage of work   (2) a strike. *See* **grève, mise à pied**

arrêté (*nm*) an order, decree, directive or by-law, issued by any of a number of bodies. *See below*

    arrêté d'insalubrité (*nm*) a certificate of unsatisfactoriness for human habitation, which entitles a property owner to an improvement grant. This is issued by the **préfet**, and entitles the occupier to a **prime à l'amélioration de l'habitat.**

arrêté ministériel (*nm*) a decision or ruling, made by a government minister, carrying the force of law

arrêté municipal (*nm*) a local by-law issued by the town hall (**mairie**)

arrêté préfectoral (*nm*) a county (or departmental) law issued by the **préfet**

arrêter les comptes (*vb*) (1) to settle an account (2) to draw up the accounts, to make up a statement of accounts

arrhes (*nf.pl*) a deposit. *See* **caution, réservation**

arrondissement (*nm*) (1) in Paris, one of the twenty numbered areas into which the city is divided. People will say, 'I live in the eighth (*le huitième*) or the twentieth (*le vingtième*).' **Arrondissements** also exist in the cities of Lyon and Marseille. (2) one of between two and six subdivisions of each **département**

artisanat (*nm*) a term referring to skilled craftsmen and craftswomen as a body

arts et métiers (*nm.pl*) (1) applied arts and crafts, design engineering (2) the name of one of the national competitive exams (**concours**), leading to a place at the **Ecole Nationale Supérieure d'Arts et Métiers**

ASSEDIC *see* **Association pour l'Emploi dans l'Industrie et le Commerce**

assemblée (*nf*) a meeting. *See* **audience**

assemblée générale annuelle (*nf*) an annual general meeting

Assemblée Nationale (*nf*) the lower house of the French parliament, sometimes called the **Chambre des Députés**. The upper house is **le Sénat**.

assiduité (*nf*) (1) regular attendance (at work, etc.) (2) punctuality. *See* **prime d'assiduité**

assiette (*nf*) the basis on which a tax rate or some other official measure is calculated or assessed. *See* **allocation de base, quotient familial**

assignation (*nf*) (1) a summons issued in a civil case, by the plaintiff to the defendant, ordering an appearance before a court to answer charges. It is often delivered by a **huissier de justice**. **assignation en justice** a writ of summons served on the defendant. **assignation à comparaître** a subpoena, an order to appear given to a witness. *See* **avenir, citation, convocation, demandeur, mise en accusation, procédure à jour, requête**

assigné/e (*nm/f*) a person summonsed to attend a court, on whom an **assignation** has been served. *See above and* **inculpé**

assigner qn (*vb*) to serve a writ on, or issue a writ against, someone. *See* **comparution, prévenu**

assimilé/e (*nm/f*) someone of comparable status to another. **les fonctionnaires et assimilés** civil servants and those in the same category. For Social Security purposes, an **assimilé** is a claimant treated as identical to a paid employee (**salarié**), though technically he or she is not.

assises (*nf.pl*) *see* **cour d'assises**

assistance (*nf*) (1) an audience, a gathering of people (2) attendance (at a meeting) (3) aid, help. *More usually* **aide** *or* **allocation**

   assistance judiciaire (*nf*) legal aid. *See* **aide judiciaire, aide légale**

   assistance publique (*nf*) (1) national assistance. **enfant de l'assistance publique** a child in care (2) the public hospital service. *See* **charge, Direction Départementale de l'Action Sanitaire et Sociale**

assister à (*vb*) to attend, be present at, witness. *See* **comparution**

association (*nf*) a society, organization or association. Any group of two or more people can set one up. If it is judged to be of public benefit (**utilité publique**) it may be entitled to a grant or tax concessions.

   association de parents d'elèves (*nf*) a parents' association (of a school)

Association des Régimes de Retraites Complémentaires (ARRCO) an association which covers complementary pension schemes like **AGIRC** below

Association Générale des Institutions de Retraite des Cadres (AGIRC) a complementary pension scheme for professional people. That is, one that adds to or tops up their State pension. *See* **cadre**

Association pour l'Emploi dans l'Industrie et le Commerce (ASSEDIC) (*nf*) the organization which oversees unemployment insurance. Employees pay around 2.5 per cent of their salary, and employers around 4.5 per cent of their wage bill, into this fund, which is a form of national insurance. All employees leaving a job should be given a certificate detailing their insurance contributions, known as an **attestation pour l'ASSEDIC.** *See* **certificat de travail**

Association pour l'Emploi des Cadres (APEC) a national organization for professional people (**cadres**)

association sportive scolaire a school sports association

associé/e (*nm/f*) a partner (in a business)

assurance (*nf*) insurance. **prendre une police d'assurance** to take out an insurance policy. *See below and* **bonus-malus, mutuelle, régime**

assurance accident du travail (*nf*) occupational injury insurance. Insurance against accidents at work

assurance au tiers (*nf*) third-party insurance

assurance auto obligatoire (*nf*) compulsory car insurance

assurance automatique acquéreur (*nf*) a form of insurance, often arranged free of charge by solicitors (**notaires**), which insures people who have signed a contract to buy land or property against having to pull out through illness, injury or death. This covers only contracts signed in the presence of a solicitor (**actes authentiques**) by a person under the age of 65, who pays a deposit of at least 5 per cent. *See* **acte authentique, acte de vente**

assurance chômage (*nf*) unemployment insurance

assurance contre le vol (*nf*) insurance against theft

assurance de responsabilité civile (*nf*) public liability or third-party insurance. It costs very little, insures for large amounts, and is often compulsory in low-risk activities such as sending a child to school. This is normally a general liability cover, and not restricted to a specific activity. However, it is used to insure motorcyclists. *See* **assurance scolaire**

assurance incendie (*nf*) fire insurance

assurance invalidité (*nf*) invalidity insurance; insurance against disablement

assurance maladie (*nf*) health insurance. *See* **ticket modérateur**

assurance maritime (*nf*) marine insurance

assurance maternité (*nf*) maternity insurance

assurance personnelle (*nf*) additional contributions paid by those (like foreign students) who are not automatically covered by the French Social Security (**Sécurité Sociale**), in order to guarantee sickness and maternity benefits

assurance responsabilité civile (*nf*) *see* **assurance de responsabilité civile**

assurance scolaire (*nf*) schoolchildren's insurance. State schools require all pupils to be insured; the sum is trifling, around £5.

assurance tertiaire (*nf*) old age pension insurance. *See also* **pension de retraite**

assurance tous risques (*nf*) fully comprehensive insurance

assurance veuvage (*nf*) widow's insurance. A contribution paid to the **Sécurité Sociale** which entitles a surviving spouse to a widow's pension for three years before the age of 55

assurance vie/assurance sur la vie (*nf*) life insurance

17

assurance vieillesse (*nf*) the state pension scheme. *See* **régime**

assurance volontaire (*nf*) additional insurance, guaranteeing old age and invalidity benefits to those who would not otherwise be entitled to them

assurances sociales (*nf.pl*) national insurance

assuré/e (*nm/f*) an insurance policy-holder, someone covered by an insurance policy (**police d'assurance**)

assuré social/assurée sociale (*nm/f*) someone covered by Social Security, i.e. a normal, paid-up member of the working population

astreindre (**qn à faire qch**) to compel, force or oblige someone to do something (in a legal sense). *See below*

astreinte (*nf*) (1) constraint, obligation   (2) a penalty, damages, often in the sense of a daily financial penalty imposed for failure to complete a contract on time. *See* **contrainte, emprise, force majeure, injonction de payer, règlement judiciaire, saisie**

atelier protégé (*nm*) a sheltered workshop, usually run by the local commune, for people who are able to work but who have physical, emotional or learning problems. *See* **Direction Départementale de l'Action Sanitaire et Sociale**

atteintes à la vie privée (nf/pl) invasion of privacy. The privacy laws in France are far stricter than in Britain, and may be invoked for relatively minor invasions of privacy. *See* **dénonciation calomnieuse**

attestation (*nf*) a certificate, attestation, an official letter confirming something. *See* **acte de notoriété, ampliation, répondant**

attestation d'acquisition (*nf*) a proof of purchase, proof of ownership. *See* **acte de vente**

attestation d'assurance (*nf*) an insurance certificate. *See* **feuille de soins**

attestation de travail (*nf*) *see* **certificat de travail**

attestation médicale (*nf*) a doctor's certificate. *See* **bon de docteur**

attestation pour l'ASSEDIC (*nf*) a certificate which an employer is obliged to give to employees on leaving their post, which is then presented to the local office of **ASSEDIC** for the purpose of assessing benefits and contributions. Similar to the British P45 scheme. *See* **certificat de travail, prestations familiales, solde de tout compte**

audience (*nf*) (1) a hearing or session (in a court case). **l'affaire vient à l'audience** the case comes before the court, the case is heard (2) an interview (for a job, etc.)

audience de jugement (*nf*) the hearing or session at the end of a court case at which the judgement is read out. *See* **séance**

audition (*nf*) (1) an audition (2) a verbal examination, verbal questioning. **l'audition des témoins** the examination of the witnesses, the part of a court case in which the witnesses give their evidence. *See* **procès-verbal**

auto-école (*nf*) a driving school. The French driving test is in two parts, one written, one practical. All learner drivers must enrol in an approved driving school in order to take the written exam. *See* **conduite accompagnée, permis de conduire**

autogestion (*nf*) collective workers' control. Literally 'self-management'

autorisation (*nf*) (1) a licence, permit (2) permission, authorization. *See* **commission rogatoire, désigné, fondé, mandement, permis, pouvoir spécial de représentation, procuration, vote par procuration**

autoroute (*nf*) a motorway, usually a toll road, designated on maps by the letter A. *See* **péage, route nationale**

auxiliaire (*nm/f*) someone employed by the State in a capacity inferior to that of a fully fledged employee (**fonctionnaire**). **Auxiliaires** do not have the same employment rights, security, career structure or pay as their colleagues. The main group is made up of **maîtres auxiliaires** in secondary schools. *See* **agent titulaire, contractuels, employé, non-titulaires**

avancement (*nm*) promotion. *See* **rétrogradation**

avantages (*nm.pl*) benefits. **avantages en nature** benefits in kind. **avantages en nature nourriture et logement** a post with board and lodging included. *See* **prestation**

avenant (*nm*) a change to a contract, an additional clause (to an insurance policy or work contract, etc.) *See* **contrat de travail, convention collective**

avenir (*nm*) a writ of summons (but one addressed by one lawyer to another, rather than served directly on a private individual by a court official). *See* **assignation, comparution**

aveu (*nm*) (1) a confession, admission   (2) testimony, a statement (to the police, etc.) *See* **audition**

avis (*nm*) (1) an opinion   (2) advice of court, a formal ruling. **rendre un avis** (of a court) to give one's views   (3) an official notice or formal order (to appear in court, etc.) *See* **comparution, radiation**

   avis de décès (*nm*) a death notice, death announcement. *See* **déclaration de non-décès, pompes funèbres**

   avis d'imposition (*nm*) a tax bill, tax reminder

   avis de réception (*nm*) an official receipt, proof of delivery, for a recorded letter. This coupon is returned to the sender after being signed by the addressee.

   avis de signification (*nm*) formal notice (of a court judgement)

avocat/e (*nm/f*) a lawyer (general term). Generally speaking, members of the public cannot represent themselves in court. Only a lawyer, registered with the local bar association (**barreau**) can do this. The main exception to this rule is the **Conseil de Prud'hommes**, even if it leads to an appeal in the **chambre sociale** of the **cour d'appel**. *See* **avoué**

avoir (*nm*) (1) assets, resources   (2) a credit note   (3) **avoir fiscal** a tax credit (on a shares dividend, used to offset tax). *See below*

avoirs (*nm.pl*)   holdings. *See* **bien, capital**

avoué/e (*nm/f*) a lawyer, working solely in a court of appeal (**cour d'appel**), as opposed to the normal lawyer or **avocat**. *See* **appel, barreau, conseiller juridique, notaire**

baccalauréat (*nm*) the baccalaureate. The French equivalent of A-levels. There are eight options (**filières**) numbered A to H, of which by far the most prestigious is **Bac C** in maths/science. The full list is: **Bac A** philosophy; **B** economics; **C** maths/science; **D** maths/natural science; **E** maths/engineering; **F** technology; **G** commerce; **H** information technology.

> **baccalauréat international** (*nm*) an internationally recognized qualification, set up and run by the **Baccalauréat International de Genève**. It is equivalent to A-levels, the French **baccalauréat**, or any similar national exam for 18-year-olds. It is recognized in many countries as a qualification for university entrance.

bachelier, bachelière (*nm/f*) someone who holds a baccalaureate

bail (*nm*) / **baux** (*nm.pl*) a lease, renting agreement (for a property, etc.) **bail commercial** a commercial lease. **donner une maison à bail** to lease out a house. **le cédant de bail** the transferrer of a lease. **prendre une maison à bail** to take out a lease on a house. *See* **location, sous-bail**

> **bail à nourriture** (*nm*) a contract in which one person promises to house and give board and lodging to someone else for the length of that person's life. This can be done either for fees, or in return for the handing over of property or other goods. *See* **obligation alimentaire, viager**

bailleur, bailleresse (*nm/f*) a lessor. The person who gives or offers a lease. *See* **locataire, propriétaire**

banque d'affaires (*nf*) a merchant bank

banque de consignation (nf) a state-run bank at which solicitors are obliged to keep clients' money, such as deposits for a house-purchase. It does *not* pay interest, either to the client or the solicitor. It guarantees that money handed over is not misused and that it will be refunded in the event of the contract falling through. *See* **notaire, promesse de vente**

banque de crédit (nf) a credit bank

banque de dépôt (nf) a deposit bank

barème (nm) a price list, a scale of charges. **barème des impôts** a tax scale, tax rates. **barème des salaires** a salary scale. *See* **honoraires**

barreau (nm) the local bar association. Only lawyers registered with the **barreau** are allowed to practise in the area covered by it. A list of members is usually displayed at the **palais de justice** and at the **Conseil de Prud'hommes**. *See* **avocat, notaire**

BAS *see* **Bureau de l'Aide Sociale**

bâteau (nm) a driveway entrance, a sloped section of pavement giving access for vehicles

bâtir (vb) to build. **terrain à bâtir** a building plot, building land. *See* **constructible, plan d'occupation des sols, servitudes, viabilisé**

bâtonnier (nm) the president of the local bar (**barreau**). *See* **avocat**

baux (nm.pl) plural of **bail**, meaning a lease

    baux commerciaux (nm.pl) commercial leasing, the renting out of a building for business purposes. This is subject to strict legal controls. *See* **fonds de commerce, franchise, plan d'occupation des sols**

    baux d'habitation (nm.pl) residential leasing, the renting out of property for people to live in

bavure (nf) an error, mistake, slip-up (usually in the sense of one made by a State employee). *See* **blâme, carence, déni de justice, forfaiture, grief, sanction administrative, suspicion légitime, tribunal administratif**

BELC *see* **Bureau pour l'Enseignement de la Langue et de la Civilisation**

BEP *see* **Brevet d'Etudes Professionnelles.** *See also* **cadre, carte professionnelle**

bibliobus (*nm*) a mobile library

bibliothèque centrale de prêt (*nf*) a central lending library in each **département**

bibliothèque municipale (*nf*) the local public library run by the **mairie**

Bibliothèque Nationale (BN) (*nf*) the National Library in Paris, equivalent to the British Library. There are a number of types of pass, typically costing around £25 in 1996. These can be difficult to obtain by people other than writers, specialists and academics. The new section of the library built at Tolbiac is intended to be more accessible to the general public.

Bibliothèque Publique d'Information (BPI) (*nf*) a large public reference library at the Beaubourg Centre in Paris

bien (*nm*) a piece of property. **biens** (*nm.pl*) (1) belongings, (personal) property (2) a fortune, estate. **Fortune** means capital, not *a* fortune in the sense of a vast amount of money. *See below and* **communauté, fortune, patrimoine, testament**

    biens communs (*nm.pl*) common or shared belongings, belongings on which two or more people have equal claim. *See* **communauté, copropriété, usufruit**

    biens corporels (*nm.pl*) tangible assets, physical property or belongings, things of value owned which can be physically seen. *See* **biens incorporels**

    biens d'équipement (*nm.pl*) capital goods

    biens et services (*nm.pl*) goods and services

    biens immeublés (*nm.pl*) fixed assets, real estate, property

    biens immobiliers (*nm.pl*) real estate, property

    biens incorporels (*nm.pl*) intangible assets, personal property that is not physical (such as a copyright)

biens meublés (*nm.pl*) movable assets, personal property

biens mobiliers (*nm.pl*) movable assets, personal property

biens publics (*nm.pl*) public property

BIJE *see* **billet international pour les jeunes**

bilan (*nm*) (1) a balance sheet, statement of accounts. **dresser son bilan** to go bankrupt   (2) an assessment. *See* **faillite, note**

bilan de liquidation (*nm*) a statement of financial situation (in bankruptcy proceedings)

billet (*nm*) (1) a ticket   (2) a banknote. *See* **bon, feuille, ticket-restaurant**

billet au porteur (*nm*) a bearer order

billet de commerce (*nm*) a promissory note

billet d'ordre (*nm*) a promissory note, bill of exchange

billet de santé (*nm*) a medical check-up

billet France vacances pass (*nm*) a rail-rover ticket allowing free travel on the **SNCF** system, for four days in a fifteen-day period, or for nine days in a calendar month. It also gives free travel on the Paris underground between the city centre and the airports, plus one other day of unlimited free travel. This pass is available only to foreigners.

billet international pour les jeunes (BIJE) (*nm*) a European rail-rover ticket for people aged under 26

bipropriété (*nf*) a form of time-sharing combined with joint ownership, in which a property or other asset (such as a boat), is split between two parties, who each have it for six months of the year. *See* **copropriété, mitoyenneté**

blâme (*nm*) disciplinary action taken against lawyers by their professional association. *See* **barreau, bavure**

blessure par imprudence (*nf*) grievous bodily harm, a category of assault, carrying a term of imprisonment of up to one year, for causing injury that leaves the victim off work for three months or more. *See* **voies de fait**

BN *see* **Bibliothèque Nationale**

boîte postale (*nf*) PO box number. *See* **poste restante**

bon (*nm*) a form, coupon, voucher, bond. *See below*

    bon de caisse (*nm*) a cash voucher

    bon de commande (*nm*) an order form

    bon de docteur (*nm*) a form signed by the social services allowing a free visit to the doctor for those on benefits or with long-term illnesses. *See* **bulletin de soins, ticket modérateur**

    bon d'épargne (*nm*) a savings certificate

    bon d'essence (*nm*) a petrol coupon, petrol voucher

    bon de garantie (*nm*) a guarantee form, guarantee slip

    bon de livraison (*nm*) a delivery slip

    bon du Trésor (*nm*) a government savings certificate

bon pour accord (*adj*) agreed to (sometimes written on the bottom of unofficial contracts, such as a letter offering a job). *See* **lu et approuvé**

bonus-malus (*nm*) a no-claims bonus on an insurance policy

bordereau (*nm*) (1) a slip, note, form (2) a statement, summary (3) an invoice (4) a document, or order, which allows a creditor to obtain money owed. *See below and* **bon, bulletin, formulaire**

    bordereau d'achat (*nm*) a purchase note

    bordereau d'envoi (*nm*) a dispatch note

    bordereau de livraison (*nm*) a delivery note

    bordereau de pièces à communiquer (*nm*) a list of the documents to be presented as evidence in a court case

    bordereau de salaire (*nm*) a salary slip, wage slip, salary advice

    bordereau de vente (*nm*) a sales invoice, note or slip. *See* **acte de vente, attestation d'acquisition**

bordereau de versement (nm) a paying-in slip

bornage (nm) a boundary-marking, especially between two properties. The act of marking would be carried out by a surveyor (**géomètre-expert**). See **mitoyenneté**

Bourse (nf) the Stock Exchange (in Paris)

bourse d'enseignement secondaire (nf) a grant for secondary education awarded to less well-off parents, or sometimes to the children themselves. This is subject to a means test. See **allocation**

bourse d'enseignement supérieur (nf) a student grant, subject to a means test and other conditions, given to students who hold the **baccalauréat** and who wish to enter higher education

bourse d'études (nf) an educational grant awarded to students for study, travel or in cases of financial hardship

BPI see **Bibliothèque Publique d'Information**

brevet (nm) (1) a licence (pilot's, etc.) (2) a patent (3) a diploma, certificate (4) the series of exams, more formally known as the **brevet des collèges**, taken at the end of the fourth year at school and equivalent to GCSE. **avoir son brevet** to have one's GCSEs. See **baccalauréat**, **Brevet d'Etudes Professionnelles**, **collège**, **lycée**

brevet d'apprentissage (nm) a certificate of apprenticeship

Brevet d'Etudes Professionnelles (BEP) (nm) a vocational qualification, inferior to a **baccalauréat** and similar to a GNVQ, awarded to 17-year-olds, which can be used either as a qualification to enter a trade or as a stepping-stone to the **baccalauréat**

brevet d'invention (nm) a patent

brigade des moeurs (nm) the vice squad

brocante (nf) (1) a (low-quality) antique shop (2) a second-hand shop (3) a flea market (4) the second-hand trade. See *below*

brocanteur/trice (nm/f) a dealer in second-hand goods or low-quality antiques. See **dépôt de vente**, **travail clandestin**

brut (*adj*) gross, as opposed to net (**net**) (of salary, etc.) *See* **cotisation**

bulletin (*nm*) (1) a form, ticket   (2) a school report   (3) a bulletin   (4) a ballot paper, voting form. *See* **bon, bordereau, formulaire**

> **bulletin de bagage** (*nm*) a luggage ticket

> **bulletin de consignation** (*nm*) a receipt given when paying a deposit on goods, such as a container for household gas, which is still widely bought in bottles. Without it you won't get your money back. *See* **caution, dépôt de garantie**

> **bulletin de consigne** (*nm*) a left-luggage ticket

> **bulletin d'état civil** (*nm*) an identity document, issued by a local authority. *See* **carte d'identité, état civil**

> **bulletin de naissance** (*nm*) a birth certificate. More commonly **extrait de naissance**

> **bulletin de paie** (*nm*) a wage slip

> **bulletin de perception** (*nm*) a tax form. *See* **avis, perception**

> **bulletin de salaire** (*nm*) a wage slip

> **bulletin de soins** (*nm*) a form signed by the social services allowing a visit to the doctor free of charge. Also known as a **bon de docteur**. *See* **feuille de soins, ticket modérateur**

> **bulletin de vote** (*nm*) a ballot paper, voting form

> **bulletin trimestriel** (*nm*) a child's termly school report

bureau (*nm*) an office. *See below*

Bureau de l'Aide Sociale (BAS) (*nm*) the local office giving out **aide sociale**

> **bureau de conciliation** (*nm*) an office at the Industrial Tribunal (**Conseil de Prud'hommes**) where, prior to the hearing of the dispute proper, an informal meeting is held in an attempt to get the two parties to settle out of court. *See* **amiable compositeur, arbitrage, bureau de jugement, conciliation, Conseil de Prud'hommes**

bureau de jugement (nm) the chamber in a court in which the case proper is heard, once preliminaries have been dealt with

bureau de l'état civil (nm) a registry office, where births, deaths, etc., are registered. Weddings, however, do not take place there. What the British call a registry-office marriage normally takes place at the town hall (**mairie**). All French marriages are secular, and conducted by the State. A church marriage is a symbolic act which, if desired, follows the civil marriage and solemnizes it. *See* **communauté**, **mariage**

bureau des hypothèques (nm) with the **cadastre**, this forms the Land Registry, but is often used as a term for the entire agency. One of its tasks is to issue lists of property transactions, so that they can be inspected by the general public.

Bureau de Vérification de la Publicité (BVP) (nm) the advertising standards authority

bureau de vote (nm) a polling station

Bureau pour l'Enseignement de la Langue et de la Civilisation (BELC) (nm) a department of the education ministry responsible for promoting the teaching of French language and culture

BVP *see* **Bureau de Vérification de la Publicité**

C

cabinet (nm) (1) a general term for the office of a professional person, e.g. a surgery or consulting room (of a doctor), chambers (of a lawyer) (2) a government minister's private office

CAC 40 France's top forty shares, listed daily at the Stock Exchange (**Bourse**)

cadastre (nm) a department of the Land Registry. *See* **bureau des hypothèques**

cadre (nm) someone with professional, managerial or executive status. It is not merely a vanity term, but entails very real advantages in terms of labour law, employment contracts, job security and improved conditions of work, and carries considerable social clout. The workforce can effectively be divided into **cadres** and the rest.

caduc (adj) null and void, not valid. *See* **nul**

caducité (nf) the state of being null and void. *See* **nullité**

cahier des charges (nm) a schedule of charges. Most commonly a list of charges, for maintenance and the like, given to someone who has bought a flat and who has to pay a percentage of the maintenance charges for the entire building in which the flat is located. The French system of buying shared property is completely different from the British. *See* **copropriété, règlement**

caisse (nf) (1) a cash desk   (2) a check-out (in a supermarket, etc.)   (3) an office, e.g. **caisse de la Sécurité Sociale** a Social Security office   (4) a cash register, till   (5) a cash-box

    caisse d'allocations familiales (nf) the family allowance department of the local Social Security office. *See* **allocation, Sécurité Sociale**

    Caisse d'Epargne et de Prévoyance (CEP) (nf) a form of state savings bank also offering life insurance, which can be found in most towns. The **CEP** is split into two halves: the **Caisse Nationale d'Epargne (CNE)**, which is the banking side; and the **Caisse Nationale de Prévoyance (CNP)**, the insurance wing.

    caisse de la Sécurité Sociale (nf) a Social Security office

candidature (nf) candidacy. **poser sa candidature à un poste** to apply for a post. *See* **à pourvoir**

cantine (nf) (1) a work canteen   (2) a refectory, school dinner hall

canton (*nm*) an electoral division for elections to the **conseil général**, made up of around a dozen **communes**. There are around ten **cantons** in each **arrondissement**, though their number and size can vary enormously.

CAP *see* **Certificat d'Aptitude Professionnelle**

CAPE *see* **Certificat d'Aptitude au Professorat d'Ecole**

CAPES *see* **Certificat d'Aptitude au Professorat de l'Enseignement du Second Degré**

CAPET *see* **Certificat d'Aptitude au Professorat de l'Enseignement Technique**

capital (*nm*) capital, funds. *See below and* **dépens**

> **capital circulant** (*nm*) working capital

> **capital décès** (*nm*) a death grant, paid by Social Security to the family of someone below retirement age who dies or is killed

> **capital d'exploitation** (*nm*) working capital

> **capital fixe** (*nm*) fixed assets, capital assets

> **capital risque** (*nm*) venture capital

> **capital social** (*nm*) company capital

CAPLP *see* **Certificat d'Aptitude au Professorat de Lycée Professionnel**

carence (*nf*) (1) bankruptcy, insolvency; the situation of someone having debts which are greater than the sum of their cash holdings or belongings. **procès-verbal de carence** bankruptcy proceedings. *See* **bilan, faillite, procès-verbal** (2) (of parents) inadequacy or neglect of children (3) (of state officials) neglect of duty resulting in prejudice to a member of the public. *See* **bavure** (4) a lack, shortcoming, lacuna (5) incompetence

carnet (*nm*) (1) a notebook (2) a book (3) an official document in book format. The word **carnet** is often used interchangeably with **carte** or **livret**. *See below*

carnet à souches (*nm*) a counterfoil book

carnet de billets (*nm*) a book of tickets (for the **métro**, etc.)
See **carte**

carnet de chèques (*nm*) a cheque-book

carnet de commande (*nm*) an order book

carnet de famille (*nm*) *same as* **livret de famille**, which is more common

carnet de maternité (*nm*) a pregnant woman's book, nursing mother's book. A book issued to an expectant mother, in which are recorded medical checks made before and after the birth. *See* **allocation, livret de famille**

carnet de notes (*nm*) a child's school report. *See* **bulletin trimestriel**

carte (*nf*) (1) a card   (2) a map   (3) a menu   (4) an official registration card. *See* **période**

carte améthyste (*nf*) a concession card for old people living in the Paris region (**Ile de France**), entitling them to reduced fares on the trains, buses and underground in and around Paris. It also gives free entry to a number of public buildings.

carte bleue (*nf*) a Visa credit card

carte Carrissimo (*nf*) a rail card for anyone under 26, giving reductions of between 20 and 50 per cent during the **période bleue**

carte couple (*nf*) a travel card for couples, of any nationality, either married or living together, giving a 50 per cent discount for the second traveller, in certain periods, on **SNCF** trains. *See* **certificat de concubinage**

carte de chemin de fer (*nf*) a railway season ticket. *See* **carte orange**

carte de circulation des non-voyants (*nf*) a travel pass for blind people in the Paris area, giving a discount for themselves and free travel for someone accompanying them

carte de combattant (*nf*) a war veteran's pass, allowing concessions across a wide range of activities, including employment and loans

carte de crédit (*nf*) a credit card

carte d'électeur (*nf*) a voter's card

carte d'étudiant (*nf*) a student's card

carte de famille nombreuse (*nf*) a pass for large families, giving reduced travel rates. It is available to parents who have five or more children, or who have three children under the age of 18 currently living with them. *See* **famille nombreuse**

carte d'identité (*nf*) a (national) identity card

carte d'identité bancaire (*nf*) a cheque card. *See* **relevé d'identité bancaire**

carte d'invalidité (*nf*) an invalidity pass, entitling the holder to a wide range of concessions in travel, housing and other areas

carte de lecteur (*nf*) a reader's card for a library, library user's card. *See* **Bibliothèque Nationale**

carte de maternité (*nf*) *same as* **carnet de maternité**

carte de résident (*nf*) a residence permit, following on from the **carte de séjour**, permitting (initially) a ten-year stay in France. After ten years it is made permanent, but can be revoked if, during the first period, the holder leaves France for more than three years.

carte de séjour (*nf*) a residence permit, sometimes called a **permis de séjour**, normally lasting from one to three years for non-EU nationals, and up to ten years for EU nationals. Non-EU nationals can only obtain this document if they already hold, or are the partner of someone holding, a **visa de long séjour**. *See* **carte de résident**

carte de travail (*nf*) *same as* **permis de travail**

carte émeraude (*nf*) an old people's or invalid's pass, issued to residents in Paris, which provides free travel, free telephone installation, free entry to facilities in Paris, plus a range of other concessions

carte grise (*nf*) a car registration book, logbook

carte kiwi (*nf*) a rail travel card for children under 16, allowing discounts for those accompanying them, plus other benefits

carte nationale d'identité (*nf*) a national identity card

carte nationale de priorité (*nf*) a priority pass, enabling queues to be jumped on transport and in various government offices. It is issued to pregnant women, and to parents with young children or with three live-in children below the age of 16.

carte orange (*nf*) a travel card, valid for one month, giving unlimited travel on the Paris transport system, whether trains or buses. Cheaper than its British equivalents, it is a must in Paris.

carte Paris famille (*nf*) a concession card for families in the Paris area who are on low incomes and who have three or more children. It entitles them to a range of grants for child care and lodging, plus free entry to facilities in Paris.

carte Paris santé (*nf*) a medical card, providing medical cover to those in the Paris area not otherwise covered

carte pastel (*nf*) a telephone card that charges calls from public call boxes directly to your account. Not a simple telephone card, which is a **télécarte**

carte professionnelle (*nf*) a card indicating membership of a professional association

carte rail Europ (*nf*) a travel card, for families or individuals, giving cut-price rail travel in several European countries

carte rubis (*nf*) a travel card for old people, giving cut-price fares on buses around Paris

carte station debout pénible (*nf*) a pass issued to people who are not strictly disabled and so who do not qualify for an invalid person's pass (**carte d'invalidité**), but who none the less find difficulty in standing. It allows them to have a seat on public transport. *See* **handicapé**

carte vermeil (*nf*) a yearly travel card for those aged 60 and over, giving concessions on **SNCF** trains and buses

cas (*nm*) a case (all senses)

cas échéant (le …) the case being, if the case arises

case (*nf*) (1) a square or compartment on a document in which details or a cross are to be written   (2) a pigeon-hole

case postale (*nf*) a post office box or pigeon-hole, in the sense of the shelf or compartment on which post is stored, as opposed to a **boîte postale**, which is the post office address box

casier de contraventions de circulation (*nm*) the national traffic offences records, which can be disclosed only to the courts and prosecuting lawyers

casier des contraventions d'alcoolisme (*nm*) a national register of alcohol-related offences, consulted by judges when passing sentence on alcohol offenders. The citizen has no right to view this file.

casier judiciaire (*nm*) the equivalent of the criminal records office, but containing details of judgements in civil as well as criminal law. The individual has a right to inspect these records. *See* **relevé de condamnation**

cassation (*nf*) *see* **cour de cassation**

cause (*nf*) (1) a cause   (2) a lawsuit, case   (3) a (lawyer's) brief. *See* **appeler**, **gain de cause**, **mise en cause**

caution (*nf*) (1) a deposit acting as a guarantee, when renting a flat, etc.   (2) security, bail. **se porter caution pour qn** to stand security for. A false friend

CCA *see* **commission des clauses abusives**

CCP *see* **compte chèques postaux**

céans (*adv*) here, in this place. An archaic term found usually in court documents

CEC *see* **collège d'enseignement secondaire**

CEDEX *see* **Courrier d'Entreprise à Distribution Exceptionnelle**

ceinture de sécurité (*nf*) a (car) seat-belt. Wearing of seat-belts is compulsory in the front seats of cars made since 1970, and in the rear of those made since 1978.

célibataire (*adj*) unmarried. *See* **communauté, concubinage**

célibataire (*nm/f*) an unmarried person

centre (*nm*) (1) centre   (2) an office. *See below*

    centre aéré (*nm*) a day centre for children of all ages, used particularly by parents who are at work during the school holidays. *See* **centre de vacances et de loisirs, colonie de vacances, crèche, halte-garderie, pouponnière**

    centre communal d'action sociale (*nm*) a community service, run by the local **commune**, to provide help for old and disabled people, and those on very low incomes. It organizes services like home help, laundry, meals, clothing and fuel. *See* **aide ménagère, allocation supplémentaire du fonds national de solidarité, recouvrement par succession**

    centre d'action culturelle (*nm*) an arts centre, subsidized by the State

    centre de documentation et d'information (CDI) (*nm*) a resource centre/library (in a school or college)

    centre de formation d'apprentis (CFA) (*nm*) a day-release college for apprentices

    centre d'information civique (CIC) (*nm*) a public information centre, but dealing with information related to elections, rather than general problems in the style of the Citizens' Advice Bureau

    centre d'information et de documentation jeunesse (CIDJ) (*nm*) an information centre for young people, dealing with careers, education, travel and leisure activities

centre d'information et d'orientation (CIO) (*nm*) a careers centre, offering guidance on jobs and training

centre de loisirs (sans hébergement) (CLSH) (*nm*) *see* **centre de vacances et de loisirs**

Centre de Recherches et d'Etudes pour la Diffusion du Français (CREDIF) (*nm*) a private organization similar to the **Alliance Française**, concerned with the teaching of French to foreigners

centre de vacances et de loisirs (*nm*) a play centre for school children during the holidays. *See* **centre aéré**

centre hospitalier (*nm*) a hospital. *See* **clinique**, **hôpital**

Centre International d'Etudes Pédagogiques (CIEP) (*nm*) a government-funded organization that promotes internationalism in education, and research into new teaching methods

centre international des étudiants et stagiaires (CIES) (*nm*) a kind of YMCA/YWCA for foreign students in France, providing lodging and advice

Centre National de Documentation Pédagogique (CNDP) (*nm*) the stationery office branch of the Ministry of Education, publishing material for the teaching profession, such as new regulations or details of the national curriculum (**tronc commun**)

Centre National d'Enseignement à Distance (CNED) (*nm*) a distance-learning organization for home study at a variety of levels

CEP *see* **certificat d'études professionnelles**

certificat (*nm*) (1) a certificate   (2) a diploma   (3) an attestation, testimonial. *See* **acte**, **attestation**, **avis**

Certificat d'Aptitude au Professorat d'Ecole (CAPE) (*nm*) an academic qualification which allows someone to become a full-status teacher in a **lycée**

Certificat d'Aptitude au Professorat de l'Enseignement du Second Degré (CAPES) (*nm*) the teaching certificate required to become a teacher in a secondary school

Certificat d'Aptitude au Professorat de l'Enseignement Technique (CAPET) (*nm*) the teaching certificate required to become a teacher of technical subjects in a secondary school

Certificat d'Aptitude au Professorat de Lycée Professionnel (CAPLP) (*nm*) the teaching qualification required of those who wish to work in a **lycée d'enseignement professionnel**

Certificat d'Aptitude Professionnelle (CAP) (*nm*) a professional, vocational qualification for those who have completed three years of study in a **lycée d'enseignement professionnel**

certificat de concubinage (*nm*) a certificate confirming that a man and woman are living together as a couple, but without being married. This is issued by the local town hall and is useful for obtaining various concessions, such as rail travel cards. *See* **carte couple**

certificat de conformité (*nm*) (1) a certificate required by the electricity board (**EDF**) before it will connect a house or flat to the mains, confirming that the wiring and equipment meet official standards (2) a certificate confirming that the building of, or alterations to, a house is not in breach of building or planning regulations

certificat d'études primaires (*nm*) a leaving certificate issued by primary schools

certificat d'études professionnelles (CEP) (*nm*) a certificate that means the opposite of what it implies, as it is awarded to those who have completed only a year in a **lycée** and who are destined for unskilled work

certificat d'immatriculation (*nm*) a certificate of registration

certificat d'investissement (*nm*) a type of inferior share, which does not confer voting rights as a full share does, and which consequently is valued at only a proportion of a full share

certificat de non-décès (*nm*) *see* **déclaration de non-décès**

certificat de perte (*nm*) a certificate issued by the police confirming that someone has reported a theft or burglary. Without this, you will not be able to claim on your insurance.

certificat de scolarité (nm) a certificate of school or university attendance. When a child is enrolled at a new school, the school will often demand written proof of previous schooling.

certificat de travail (nm) a certificate given by employers to employees leaving their posts, which confirms the name, duties and length of service in the position. A new employer usually demands to see it before confirming an offer of employment and may refuse to give a promised contract if it is not produced. See **attestation pour l'ASSEDIC, engagement de non-concurrence**

certificat d'urbanisme (nm) the official reply to a planning search put in by those intending to buy land or property. It gives details of the services available on the property and of future developments that might affect it. See **permis de construire, plan d'occupation des sols, servitudes, urbanisme**

CES see **collège d'enseignement secondaire**

cessation (nf) cessation, suspension, stopping. See **arrêt de travail, grève, licenciement, mise à pied**

cessation d'activité (nf) cessation of business. See **bilan**

cessation de travail (nf) stoppage of work. See **arrêt de travail**

cession-bail (nf) the leasing back of a property to the seller, by the buyer to whom it was sold. See **fonds de commerce, rente viagère**

cession de parts (nf) transfer of shares

CFA see **centre de formation d'apprentis**

CFDT see **Confédération Française Démocratique du Travail**

CFTC see **Confédération Française des Travailleurs Chrétiens**

CGC see **Confédération Générale des Cadres**

CGPME *see* **Confédération Générale des Petites et Moyennes Entreprises**

CGT *see* **Confédération Générale du Travail**

chambre (*nf*) (1) a bedroom　(2) a division or chamber (of a court, etc.)

> **chambre civile** (*nf*) a chamber of the **cour de cassation** or the **tribunal de grande instance** covering matters that fall under civil law (**droit privé**)

> **chambre correctionnelle** (*nf*) *same as* **tribunal correctionnel**

> **chambre d'accusation** (*nf*) a court of criminal appeal

> **chambre de commerce et d'industrie** (*nf*) a chamber of commerce, of which there is at least one in every **département**

> **Chambre des Députés** (*nf*) *see* **Assemblé Nationale**

> **chambre des métiers** (*nf*) a kind of local chamber of commerce, at **département** level, representing the interests of craftsmen and women

> **chambre des mises en accusation** (*nf*) a court which holds preliminary hearings, following the investigations of a **juge d'instruction**. Its purpose is to decide if there is a case to answer and if the accused (**inculpé**) is to be formally charged (made an **accusé**) and brought before the assizes (**cour d'assises**).

> **chambre des requêtes** (*nf*) a court of civil appeal

> **chambre sociale** (*nf*) a court, or section, of the **palais de justice** dealing with civil disputes, or with appeals against decisions by the Industrial Tribunal. *See* **Conseil de Prud'hommes**

changement de résidence (*nm*) change of address

charge (*nf*) (1) tax burden, tax liability　(2) a responsibility, office. **à la charge de** (a) to be charged to (of costs, expenses, etc.)　(b) in the care of, under the control of (the social services, etc.) *See below and* **Direction Départementale de l'Action Sanitaire et Sociale**

charge publique (*nf*) public office

charges (*nf.pl*) (1) expenses, outgoings, costs (2) charges brought in court (3) service charges (see **cahier, frais, honoraires**)

charges d'exploitation (*nf.pl*) operating expenses. *See* **exploitation**

charges familiales (*nf.pl*) family living expenses or outgoings. Also called **charges de famille**. *See* **déclaration de ressources**

charges financières (*nf.pl*) financing costs, outlay

charges locatives (*nf.pl*) maintenance or service charges on rented accommodation. *See* **cahier des charges, copropriété**

charges sociales (*nf.pl*) the total deductions from salary covering national insurance, social security and the like. *See* **cotisation**

chef (*nm*) (1) a boss, head, the most senior person (at work) (2) right, legal title. **du chef de son mari** in one's husband's right (3) headings, categories (on an official form). **les chefs de la demande** the list of charges (in a civil court case). **les chefs d'accusation** the list of charges

chef d'entreprise (*nm*) a company manager or director

chef de famille (*nm*) the head of the family (for tax and other official purposes)

chef d'inculpation (*nm*) a list of charges (brought in court), an indictment

chef lieu (*nm*) the equivalent of a county town. In a **département** this is the town where the **préfet**'s office is located, in an **arrondissement** the town of the **sous-préfet**'s office.

chefs de la demande (*nm.pl*) a list of charges, claims or demands (as made by the plaintiff in a court case for example). *See* **bordereau**

chemin communal (*nm*) (1) an unclassified road (2) a public right of way. *See* **bornage, droit de passage**

cheptel (nm) livestock. In legal proceedings **cheptel mort** refers to implements or other equipment belonging to a farm, **cheptel vif** to livestock and animals.

chèque (nm) (1) a cheque　(2) a voucher, see **ticket-restaurant**

chèque au porteur (nm) a cheque to bearer

chèque barré (nm) a crossed cheque

chèque certifié (nm) a certified cheque

chèque de banque (nm) a bank draft. Unlike its English equivalent, this cannot be used as cash, but must first be cleared like a normal cheque. A false friend

chèque de voyage (nm) a traveller's cheque

chèque en blanc (nm) a blank cheque

chèque essence (nm) a petrol coupon or voucher

chèque non-barré (nm) an uncrossed cheque

chèque postal (nm) a post office giro cheque

chèque-repas (nm) same as **chèque-restaurant**

chèque-restaurant (nm) a luncheon voucher. See **ticket-restaurant**

chèque sans provision (nm) a bad or bouncing cheque. It is illegal in France to issue a cheque for which there are insufficient funds. Anyone receiving one has the right to take the sender to court at the **tribunal de grande instance**. The bank itself will impose a one-month ban on issuing cheques for a first offence, rising to twelve months for a second. See **compensable**

chèque-vacances (nm) a holiday voucher, issued to workers by the employer, and redeemable when booking holidays through a travel agent

chéquier (nm) a cheque-book

chevaux (CV) (nm.pl) horsepower or c.c. (of a car, etc.). The unit of power in which engine capacity is measured

chômage (nm) unemployment. **être au chômage** to be out of work. *See* **licenciement**

chômeur/chômeuse (nm/f) an unemployed person

CHSCT *see* **comité d'hygiène, de sécurité et des conditions de travail**

CIC *see* **centre d'information civique**

CIDEX *see* **Courrier Individu(el) à Distribution Exceptionnelle**

CIDJ *see* **centre d'information et de documentation de jeunesse**

CIEP *see* **Centre International d'Etudes Pédagogiques**

CIES *see* **centre international des étudiants et stagiaires**

ci-joint (adj/adv) included, attached, enclosed. **veuillez trouver ci-joint** please find enclosed. *See* **annexe, avenant**

CIO *see* **centre d'information et d'orientation**

citation (nf) a summons to appear in court (for either a defendant or a witness). *See below and* **assigner, comparution**

    citation à comparaître (nf) a summons to appear before a court, either as accused or as witness

    citation directe (nf) a summons to appear before a (criminal) court

    citation en justice (nf) a summons

cité (nf) a city. **cité administrative** the buildings where the government services are housed. **cité universitaire** student residences attached to a university

citer (vb) (1) to summons (a defendant to appear in a court) (2) to subpoena (a witness)

citer devant un tribunal (vb) to summon someone to appear before a court

clandestin (adj) *see* **travail clandestin**

classe (nf) a class. The numbering of classes in French secondary schools runs opposite to that in Britain: first year in secondary school is the sixth (**sixième** or **classe de sixième**), progressing to the final year (**classe terminale**), in which the **baccalauréat** is taken. **Classe préparatoire** is a post-baccalaureate course of two years, which prepares the most able students for the competitive exams (**concours**) for entrance to the best universities (*see* **grande école**).

classe de neige (*nf*) a school trip to a ski resort, to allow children to combine schoolwork with ski tuition

classe terminale (*nf*) final year, mainly used of 17- to 18-year-olds in their last year at school, when they take the **baccalauréat**. Also used for final year of courses generally. See **école**

clause de non-concurrence (*nf*) *see* **engagement de non-concurrence**

clause suspensive (*nf*) *see* **alinéa**, **engagement de non-concurrence**

client (*nm*) a client, customer, guest (in a hotel)

clinique (*nf*) (1) a private hospital, nursing home, private clinic; **clinique** normally refers to a private establishment, **hôpital** to a public one   (2) (within a public hospital) a clinic

clinique d'accouchement (*nf*) a maternity home

clôture (*nf*) (1) closing, closure (**clôture annuelle** annual closure or holidays)   (2) a fence or boundary wall   (3) the act (or right) of fencing off property. Shared boundaries can be a complex issue in buying property in France. *See* **bornage**

CNDP *see* **Centre National de Documentation Pédagogique**

CNE (Caisse Nationale d'Epargne) *see* **Caisse d'Epargne et de Prévoyance**

CNED *see* **Centre National d'Enseignement à Distance**

CNP (Caisse Nationale de Prévoyance) *see* **Caisse d'Epargne et de Prévoyance**

CNPF *see* **Confédération Nationale du Patronat Français**

cocher (d'une croix) (*vb*) to mark with a cross (on official documents). *See* **case**

co-contractant (*nm*) the second party involved in signing a contract. *See* **cosignataire**

code (*nm*) (1) a code   (2) a law   (3) a code of law. *See below*

> **code de déontologie** (*nm*) a rule book

> **code de la route** (*nm*) the highway code. **rouler en code** to drive with dipped headlights

> **code départemental** (*nm*) a county or departmental law, as opposed to a national or local one. *See* **arrêt**, **département**

Code (*nm*) national law. France is a very rule-minded society. There are many **codes** (published by Dalloz in dense, red volumes) explaining the duties and obligations of the citizen in almost every circumstance. The most important **codes** are:

> **Code Civil** (*nm*) the collected laws relating to civil law

> **Code Pénal** (*nm*) the collected laws relating to criminal law

> **Code du Travail** (*nm*) the collected laws relating to employment law, including conditions of employment and the correct procedure for hiring and firing staff

Other **codes** are:

> **Code Administratif** (*nm*) administrative law, covering the duties of civil servants

> **Code de Commerce** (*nm*) commercial law

> **Code de la Construction et de l'Habitation** (*nm*) housing and construction law

> **Code de l'Environnement** (*nm*) environmental law

> **Code de Justice Militaire** (*nm*) military law

> **Code de la Nationalité** (*nm*) citizenship and immigration law

> **Code de Procédure Civile** (*nm*) now **Nouveau Code de Procédure Civile** the law of civil procedure (for courts, tribunaux, etc.)

> **Code de Procédure Pénale** (*nm*) prison law

> **Code de la Santé Publique, de la Famille et de l'Aide Sociale**

(nm) the law relating to public health, the family and social welfare

Code de la Sécurité Sociale, Code de la Mutualité, Mutualité Sociale Agricole (nm) social security and benefits law

Code de l'Urbanisme (nm) the law relating to development and town planning

Code des Loyers et de la Copropriété (nm) the law relating to rents and the joint ownership of property

Code des Sociétés (nm) company law

Code Electoral (nm) electoral law

Code Forestier (nm) forestry law

Code Général des Impôts (nm) tax law

Code Rural (nm) the law of the countryside

CODEVI see **Compte pour le Développement Industriel**

coefficient d'occupation du sol (COS) (nm) a formula which determines the maximum legal size of a building relative to the size of the plot on which it stands

coefficient familial (nm) family rating. Like a tax code, it is a score or formula, worked out on the basis of income and expenditure, which determines how well off a family is and what concessions it is entitled to in matters like paying for school dinners.

collaborateur/collaboratrice (nm/f) (1) a work colleague (2) an assistant, particularly in the sense of a (foreign) personal assistant to a company executive (3) (*pejorative*) a collaborator with the Nazis during World War II

collatéral/collatéraux (nm.sing/pl) collateral, money lent or offered as security to guarantee a loan

collège (nm) the normal title for the state school attended by all children aged 11 to 15. At 15 they move on to a **lycée**, which is roughly equivalent to a sixth-form college.

collège d'enseignement secondaire (CES) (nm) a now obsolete term for a secondary school. *See above*

colonie de vacances (*nf*) a summer camp for children during the holidays. *See* **centre aéré**

comité d'entreprise (*nm*) an employees' consultative committee, or works council, obligatory in businesses employing more than fifty people, and made up of the employer or his or her delegate, and representatives elected by union members. These are meant to discuss issues related to employment, in particular conditions of work. In businesses with fewer than ten employees, this committee is replaced by the **délégués du personnel**, who are delegates elected by a vote of all the workers.

comité d'hygiène, de sécurité et des conditions de travail (CHSCT) (*nm*) a workers' committee, compulsory in businesses employing more than fifty people, which consults with the employer on matters relating to health, safety and conditions of work

commandant de police (*nm*) (1) a commander, commandant (of a police station) (2) a major in the army, a squadron leader in the airforce. *See* **commissaire de police**

commissaire de police (*nm*) a senior, plain-clothes police officer in the **police nationale**, equivalent in rank to a British superintendent

commissaire du gouvernement (*nm*) a judge appointed to examine a case and to present and discuss the options open to fellow judges. *See* **juge**, **magistrat**, **tribunal**

commissaire-priseur (*nm*) an auctioneer. In France auctioneers belong to a professional body to which entry is strictly controlled by examination. *See* **salle des ventes**

commissariat de police (*nm*) a police station, under the command of a **commissaire de police**. *See* **bureau**, **hôtel**, **police**, **préfecture**

commission (*nf*) (1) a commission, council, committee. **travailler à la commission** to work on commission

    commission d'arbitrage (*nf*) an arbitration committee. A group of people who try to resolve disputes between individuals, or between an employer and employee(s), in an effort to avoid the matter going to court or the industrial tribunal. *See below and* **Conseil de Prud'hommes**

commission de conciliation (*nf*) a conciliation service open to the general public, which attempts to settle disputes, such as those between a landlord and tenant, without the need to resort to a court (**tribunal d'instance**). *See above and* **amiable compositeur, arbitrage, conciliateur, conciliation**

commission des clauses abusives (CCA) (*nf*) a kind of office of fair trading for contracts, a consumer watchdog, set up by the government, to which people can complain about clauses and small print in contracts or order forms which they feel are dishonest

commission d'office (*nf*) the appointment of counsel by a court

commission rogatoire (*nf*) letters rogatory; a warrant signed by a judge giving authority to a state official, such as a police officer, to carry out certain actions on the court's behalf. *See* **autorisation, mandement, mise en accusation, perquisition**

Commission Technique d'Orientation et de Reclassement Professionnel (COTOREP) (*nf*) a disability board, which classes disabled workers and their allowances according to the degree of disability

communauté (*nf*) (1) a community (2) a marriage contract. Marriage in France can be a very legalistic event, involving one of the many marriage contracts listed below. *See below and* **concubinage, conjoint, dispense de bans, donation entre époux, examen médical prénuptial, extrait d'acte de mariage, livret de famille, mariage, régime matrimonial, séparation des biens, union libre**

communauté d'acquêts (*or* **régime de la communauté d'acquêts**) (*nf*) a contract in which there is common ownership of possessions acquired after the marriage takes place, but in which each partner retains sole possession of anything acquired before it. This is the standard practice, and is assumed to apply unless an agreement to the contrary is drawn up. Sometimes called **communauté de la participation aux acquêts** or **communauté réduite aux acquêts**

communauté de meubles et d'acquêts (régime de la ...) (nf) a contract in which both partners retain sole possession of properties and real estate – but not other possessions – acquired both before and during the marriage

communauté de la séparation des biens (régime de la ...) (nf) a contract in which both partners own their possessions separately. The opposite of a **communauté universelle**

communauté entre époux (régime de la ...) (nf) the holding of a joint estate between a man and his wife

communauté légale (régime de la ...) (nf) a marriage without a formal marriage contract, in which a couple agree to hold some goods jointly, while others are owned by each partner separately. See **concubinage**

communauté réduite aux acquêts (régime de la ...) (nf) *same as* **communauté d'acquêts**

communauté universelle (régime de la ...) (nf) a contract in which all the couple's belongings are owned jointly

communauté urbaine (nf) a federation of **communes** joining forces to provide better planning or services. See **agglomération**

commune (nf) a small community similar to a parish, and equivalent to a rural district if in the country or a borough if in a town. The **commune** is the basic unit in French administration, and can vary in size from an entire town to a village, hamlet or knot of houses. It has a **mairie** and a **conseil municipal**. Each **commune** is part of a group forming a **canton**. See **arrondissement**, **département**

communication (nf) disclosure (in a court case). The sending of documents by one party to the other. In French court cases, each side must disclose its evidence and arguments to the opposition before the case comes to court. The **communication**

de pièces is the stage preceding the hearing at which the defendant and plaintiff exchange legal dossiers (**dossiers**).

communiquer (*vb*) to send, transmit

Compagnie des Eaux (*nf*) a water company. *See* **service des eaux**

Compagnies Républicaines de Sécurité (CRS) (*nf.pl*) a division of the **police nationale** specializing in riot control and public order maintenance. They are military in appearance, renowned for their aggression, and remembered for their suppression of the 1968 riots and more recent football ground disturbances. *See* **gendarme, police nationale**

comparaître (*vb*) to appear before a court. *See* **comparution** *and* **non-comparution**

comparution (*nf*) a formal appearance before a court or similar body. *See* **citation, convocation**

compensable (*adj*) (of a cheque) able to be cleared; (a cheque) for which there are sufficient funds. *See* **chèque sans provision**

compétence (*nf*) (1) skill, ability, competence (to do something) (2) competence, jurisdiction (in law). **la compétence prud'hommale** the legal competence of the Industrial Tribunal. *See* **juridiction**

complément familial (*nm*) a kind of family income supplement paid to those on low incomes with three or more children. *See* **aide, allocation**

compositeur *see* **amiable compositeur**

compris (*adj*) included. **TTC: toutes taxes comprises** all tax (VAT) included

compromis de vente (*nm*) an agreement to buy and sell; a form of pre-contract, when the buyer and seller make a written agreement, but prior to the signing of the sale contract proper. Also known as **promesse de vente avec dédit** and **promesse de vente synallagmatique**. *See* **acte authentique, acte de vente, acte sous-seing privé, contrat de réservation, promesse**

comptabilité (*nf*) (1) (the profession of) accountancy (2) accounts, bookkeeping (3) accountant's or bookkeeper's office

comptabilité des sociétés (*nf*) company accounts, the firm's books

comptable (*nm*) an accountant

compte (*nm*) a term used in conjunction with other words, but not on its own, to signify a bank account. The principal types of account are listed below. **avoir un compte à découvert** to have an overdraft. *See* **compensable**

compte à terme (*nm*) an interest-paying deposit account, in which a certain number of days' notice must be given in order to withdraw funds

compte bancaire (*nm*) a bank account

compte bloqué (*nm*) a frozen account

compte chèques postaux (CCP) (*nm*) a current account run by the post office (**PTT**)

compte courant (*nm*) a current account. *See* **compte de dépôts**

compte créditeur (*nm*) a credit account. *See* **solde**

compte de dépôts (*nm*) a current account. The most common form of bank account, with a cheque-book and allowing immediate withdrawal of money

compte épargne-logement (*nm*) a savings account (tax-free) with a bank or other institution, which after a short period allows the depositor to apply for a mortgage or home-improvement loan

compte odysée (*nm*) a young person's (under 18) version of the **compte chèques postaux**

Compte pour le Développement Industriel (CODEVI) (*nm*) a fixed-rate investment account in a bank or post office, linked to industrial development in France

compte sur livret (*nm*) a savings account, using a passbook instead of a cheque-book

concessionnaire (*nm*) an authorized agent or dealer, franchise holder, concessionnaire. *See* **franchise**

concierge (nm/f) the caretaker of a building or block of flats. A position of considerable power and responsibility. Nowadays **gardien/gardienne** is more commonly used.

conciliateur (nm) someone who arbitrates in disputes in an effort to resolve them without the need for court action. *See* **amiable compositeur, arbitrage, conciliation**

conciliation (nf) conciliation, dispute settling. *See* **amiable compositeur, arbitrage, bureau de conciliation, commission de conciliation, conciliateur, séance**

conclure un contrat (vb) to enter into a contract or agreement with someone

conclusions (nf.pl) (1) a summing up, winding-up speech in court proceedings by a judge or lawyer (2) pleadings, submission, the arguments put forward by either party in a civil court case (3) verdict, findings (of a jury or inquiry). *See* **communication de pièces**

concours (nm) a competitive examination. Entry to the **grandes écoles** and to the professions (and promotion within them) is often controlled by highly competitive exams. Ostensibly concerned with maintaining standards, the exams have a narrow scope, with the side-effect of making it difficult for outsiders and foreigners to break in, particularly when some exams can be sat only by those with specific qualifications. Teaching is one such profession. *See below and* **engagement de non-concurrence, équivalence**

> **concours externe** (nm) a competitive examination for outsiders trying to get into a profession

> **concours de la Fonction Publique** (nm) a competitive examination for entry to the Civil Service. The equivalent of the British Civil Service examination. *See* **l'Administration**

> **concours général** (nm) a prestigious academic competition for schoolchildren, with prizes in various subjects, open to the most able students in the final year (**classe terminale**) or next-to-final year (*classe de première*) at state-run secondary schools (**lycées**). *See* **classe, école**

concours interne (nm) a competitive examination for promotion, open to those already in a profession

concubinage (nm) cohabitation, a couple living together as man and wife without going through a formal marriage ceremony. **concubinage notoire** common-law marriage. Cohabiting couples are entitled to certain benefits, including travel concessions, if they produce a **certificat de concubinage** confirming their status. **vivre en concubinage** to live together as man and wife. See **carte couple, communauté, union libre**

concurrence (nf) competition. See **engagement de non-concurrence**

conditions de ressources (nf.pl) financial means or resources

conduite accompagnée (CA) (nf) accompanied driving. Much stricter than in Britain, this is a formal system of learning to drive, recognized by insurance companies, in which *certain* kinds of qualified driver are allowed to accompany *certain* kinds of unqualified ones. The accompanied must be 16 or over and have passed the written part of the test. The accompanying driver must be over 28, with three years' experience and no major endorsements. See **auto-école, permis de conduire**

Confédération Française Démocratique du Travail (CFDT) (nf) one of the largest trade-union organizations, drawn mainly from blue-collar workers. It is socialist in policy and advocates workers' control of industry.

Confédération Française des Travailleurs Chrétiens (CFTC) (nf) another large trade-union organization with members of all types, marked by a commitment to Christian – usually Catholic – values

Confédération Générale des Cadres (CGC) (nf) a private-sector union representing professional, executive and managerial staff (**cadres**)

Confédération Générale des Petites et Moyennes Entreprises (CGPME) (nf) an organization representing small employers. It is part of the **Confédération Nationale du Patronat Français**.

Confédération Générale du Travail (CGT) (nf) France's most important union, representing workers in large, mainly nationalized, industries such as the railways. It is communist-leaning.

Confédération Nationale du Patronat Français (CNPF) (nf) a confederation speaking for a number of different employers' organizations, which stages national conferences, publicity campaigns and the lobbying of politicians. It is made up of a number of more specialized employers' organizations such as the **Confédération Générale des Petites et Moyennes Entreprises.** See **patronat**

Confédération Paysanne (nf) a peasant farmers' organization

conformément à (prep) in accordance with, in conformity with (the law, etc.)

conformité (nf) conformity. **attestation de conformité** a certificate issued by **CONSUEL**, the National Safety Council for Electricity Users, which confirms that the wiring in a property meets the required standard, and which the Electricity Board, **EDF**, may wish to see before connecting or reconnecting supplies

confort acoustique (nm) the **certificat de confort acoustique** is a guarantee of sound-proofing offered with newly built properties

congé (nm) (1) holidays, vacation. **préavis de congé** notice of intention to take a holiday   (2) leave, time off (from work). **congé sans traitement** unpaid leave   (3) notice to quit or leave. **donner son congé** to hand in one's notice. **donner un congé à qn** to give someone notice to leave (an employee, a tenant, etc.). See **licenciement** (4) a clearance certificate (e.g. allowing goods to be removed from customs)

congé annuel (nm) annual holidays or leave (from work)

congé d'enseignement et de recherche (nm) unpaid leave for employees with a minimum of two years' service with their employer, for purposes of further training. See **congé sabbatique**

congé de formation (nm) further training leave. An employee with a minimum of six months' service with the current employer and two years' employment experience in his or her field is entitled to a period of leave for further training, for which part wages are paid.

congé de maladie (nm) sick leave. See **feuille de soins**

congé de maternité (nm) (paid) maternity leave. This can vary from 16 to 26 weeks, depending on the number of previous children.

congé parental d'éducation (nm) unpaid leave for the purpose of looking after a child under the age of 3. All employees are legally entitled to this.

congé(s) payé(s) (nm) paid leave. This amounts to two and a half days for each month worked that year. Every employee is entitled to this by law.

congé sabbatique (nm) sabbatical leave, unpaid, to which any employee having at least six years' experience in his or her field and at least three years' service with the present employer is entitled. This leave can be taken once in every six-year cycle.

congés scolaires (nm.pl) school holidays. See **rentrée**

congédier (vb) to give someone notice to leave (of an employee given his or her cards, or a tenant ordered to leave a rented property)

conjoint/conjointe (nm/f) a spouse; husband or wife. **conjoints futurs** the bride- and groom-to-be, an engaged couple. See **communauté**

conseil (nm) (1) a council, tribunal, committee   (2) an adviser, lawyer   (3) a piece of advice

conseil d'administration (nm) board of directors, board of governors, management committee

conseil d'arrondissement (nm) the local council, elected to serve an **arrondissement**

conseil de classe (nm) (1) a staff meeting (in a school) (2) a class committee made up of students, teachers and parents (in a **collège** or **lycée**)

Conseil d'Etat (nm) an advisory body consisting of around 200 experts, which sits in judgement on administrative law and gives advice to parliament on the effects of proposed legislation

conseil de famille (nm) a formal meeting of members of a family, to deal with legal matters like the reading of wills

conseil des maîtres (nm) teachers' committee in an **école primaire**

conseil des professeurs (nm) a teachers' committee in a **collège** or **lycée**

Conseil de Prud'hommes (nm) an industrial tribunal. Its services are free, and it is empowered to enforce the law or grant compensation in disputes between employers and employees. It does not give advice. *See* **arbitrage, conciliation, Inspection du Travail, licenciement, maison de l'avocat**

conseil général (nm) the council of a **département**, roughly equivalent to a county council in Britain

conseil juridique (nm) *see* **conseiller juridique**

conseil municipal (nm) the local council of a **commune**, elected for six years and electing in turn the mayor (**maire**)

conseil régional (nm) roughly equivalent to a county council. The council elected to serve a **département**

conseil syndical (nm) a management committee in a block of flats, made up of the flats' owners. This looks after general matters of policy, including aspects of maintenance, but is generally separate from the day-to-day running, which is handled by an agent or manager (**gérant d'immeuble**). *See* **cahier des charges, concierge, copropriété, fonds de roulement, syndic d'immeuble**

conseiller/conseillère (nm/f) (1) a counsellor, adviser (2) a (town) councillor   (3) a judge in a higher court, such as the **cour d'appel**, **cour de cassation** or **Conseil d'Etat**. *See below*

> **conseiller d'éducation** (*nm*) a type of school marshal in a **collège** or **lycée**, responsible for discipline and truancy problems

> **conseiller de la mise en état** (*nm*) a judge in an appeal court (**cour d'appel**) who carries out at the higher level the same role of preparing the groundwork for complex cases that is performed in the lower courts by a **juge de la mise en état**. *See* **cours**, **juge**

> **conseiller d'orientation** (*nm*) a careers adviser

> **conseiller juridique** (*nm*) a legal adviser. Someone specializing in consultations and advice on specific areas of law. Also able to draw up an **acte sous-seing privé**, he or she can assist or represent clients before certain kinds of hearing or authorities, such as commercial courts. *See* **tribunal de commerce**

> **conseiller matrimonial** (*nm*) a marriage guidance counsellor

> **conseiller technique** (*nm*) a technical adviser

consentement (*nm*) consent, agreement. *See* **vice**, **nul**

consentir un prêt (*vb*) to agree to or grant a loan

conserver (*vb*) to keep. **à conserver impérativement** to be retained (of receipt, etc.)

consigne (*nf*) (1) a deposit (on a gas bottle, etc.)   (2) a left-luggage office. **consigne automatique** left-luggage lockers   (3) instructions, orders

constat (*nm*) a formal, certified report, such as an inventory of house contents, a damage report, or a log of antisocial behaviour by the neighbours. This can be drawn up by a **huissier**, to add legal weight and credibility to any formal complaint or insurance claim. A **constat amiable** is a similar, but informal statement, drawn up amicably between two parties in a dispute. *See* **amiable**

constructible (*adj*) with building permission (of land which has been passed for building on by the local authorities). However, what is built on it may still be subject to restrictions. *See* **certificat d'urbanisme, copropriété, viabilisé**

CONSUEL the electricity users' national safety council. *See* **conformité**

contentieux (*nm*) court case, litigation, legal action, often in the broader sense of the totality of matters able to be examined by a given judge or court. For example, **le contentieux administratif** legal matters falling within the jurisdiction of administrative law, whether in a **tribunal** or appeal court. *See* **action, affaire, ester en justice, justice**

contourner (*vb*) to circumvent, bend or get round (the law or a rule). *See* **système D**

contracter un emprunt (*vb*) to take out a loan

contractuels/elles (*nm/f.pl*) workers like **auxiliaires**, with inferior rights and job security, employed by the state on fixed contracts rather than in permanent posts as **fonctionnaires**

contradictoire (*adj*) is a false friend. A **jugement contradictoire** is a judgement in a court case given after due hearing of both parties. *See* **appel, jugement en premier ressort** (*at* **ressort**)

contraignant (*adj*) binding, constraining, restricting

contrainte (*nf*) constraint or coercion. Forcing someone to act against their will, whether by physical or more subtle kinds of pressure. Any contract, including a contract of employment, signed where pressures of this kind are present, is invalid. *See* **caduc, dol, nul**

contrat (*nm*) a contract, agreement. **passer un contrat avec** to sign a contract with. *See below and* **acte authentique, acte sous-seing privé, compromis de vente, promesse, sous-traité**

> **contrat d'abonnement** (*nm*) (1) a rental agreement (2) a subscription (3) a season ticket

> **contrat de fonction** (*nm*) a service contract

> **contrat de location** (*nm*) a lease, rental agreement, contract to rent (a property, etc.). *See* **sous-bail**

contrat de réservation (*nm*) a contract, or rather a pre-contract (**contrat préliminaire**), promising to buy a property still in the process of being built. This is common with flats, and to a lesser extent with houses. It allows the buyer to pay over a longer period and to have some say in interior decoration and layout. A deposit of 2 to 5 per cent is required if the period of building is less than two years, no deposit if it is greater. If the **contrat de réservation** is not signed in a **notaire**'s office, there is a seven-day cooling-off period for the buyer to back out. *See* **compromis de vente, délai de réflexion, état futur d'achèvement, indemnité d'immobilisation, provision**

contrat de travail (*nm*) a contract of employment. Employment practice in France is complex and rigid, containing many pitfalls for unwary foreigners. It is advisable to accept no job offer without first having a written contract in hand, and to consult a specialist on French law before signing it. *See below and* **convention collective, engagement de non-concurrence, licenciement, publicité mensongère, travail, vacation**

contrat de travail à durée déterminée (*nm*) the more common term for a temporary post, in the sense of a fixed-term contract of employment. This can be renewed twice only. *See* **travail temporaire**

contrat de travail à durée indéterminée (*nm*) a permanent contract of employment

contrat synallagmatique (*nm*) a bilateral or reciprocal contract, in which both parties undertake a certain duty. All house purchases come into this category, as one party agrees to supply the property, the other the money to buy it.

contrat verbal (*nm*) a verbal contract. France is the land of the written word. Verbal promises and contracts are highly irregular and no French person would dream of accepting one on any matter of importance. Their existence can be difficult to prove in court without some kind of *written* evidence (e.g a wage slip to prove that an offer of work had been made).

contravention (*nf*) (1) a fine (2) an offence of a minor type, like a parking violation, often punished by a fixed penalty. *See* **amende forfaitaire, délit, infraction**

contrefaçon (*nf*) (1) a forgery, counterfeiting (2) an unauthorized or pirate copy. *See* **ampliation**

contrefaire (*vb*) to forge, counterfeit

contribuable (*nm/f*) a taxpayer, someone who pays tax contributions

contrôlable (*adj*) to be retained for inspection. **un billet contrôlable à l'arrivée** a ticket to be retained for inspection at the destination

contrôle (*nm*) formal inspection or checking (of papers, tickets, etc.)

    contrôle d'identité (*nm*) a check of identity papers

    contrôle technique (*nm*) an MOT test

contrôler (*vb*) to inspect or check (papers, tickets, etc.)

contrôleur (*nm*) a ticket inspector

convention collective (*nf*) a collective agreement drawn up between employers and workers. Ostensibly to allow conditions of employment more 'flexible' than those laid down in the **Code du Travail**, in practice they often impose hours and conditions of work greatly inferior to the norm in the occupation. They are common in schools of English as a Foreign Language, one of the few areas where foreign teachers can find work. Details of the changes allowed are rarely given in a work contract, even though they may permit duties and working conditions different from those written on the contract itself. The existence, name and reference number of the agreement in question should be stated on the work contract and a copy of the agreement displayed in the place of work. *See* **amplitude journalière, publicité mensongère, roulement, travail à quart**

conventionné (*adj*) (of a hospital) National Health, as opposed to private

conventionnel (*adj*) contractual, relating to a contract

convocation (*nf*) (1) a formal summons to appear, notification to attend (a court, police station, interview, etc.) (2) a convening (of a meeting). *See* **assignation, avis, demande**

convoquer (*vb*) to summon someone to appear before (*devant*) (a court, etc.)

coordonnées (*nf.pl*) name, address and telephone number. To ask for someone's **coordonnées** is the commonest way of asking for this information.

copie (*nf*) a copy (of a document, etc.). *See* **ampliation**

> **copie certifiée conforme** (*nf*) a certified copy. *See* **acte de notoriété, ampliation**

copropriété (*nf*) co-ownership, of land, buildings and other assets such as a flat or boat. This is a much more common practice than in Britain, particularly when buying a flat. In France, the buyer purchases not a lease from the owner of the block of flats, but a part-share in the entire building. *See* **cahier des charges, démembrement de propriété, règlement, syndicat**

correctionnel/le (*adj*) refers to a criminal court (concerned with **délits**)

correctionnelle (passer en ...) (*vb*) to appear before a criminal court

COS *see* **coefficient d'occupation du sol**

cosignataire (*nm/f*) a co-signatory, the other person in the signing of a contract. *See* **co-contractant**

cotisation (*nf*) subscription, contributions, dues, deductions (out of wages, etc.)

COTOREP *see* **Commission Technique d'Orientation et de Reclassement Professionnel**

coupable (*adj*) guilty. *See* **accusé, inculpé**

Cour (la) (*nf*) the Bench, term of address for the judges in a court case

cour (*nf*) a court, but usually of a higher, specialist type. Courts in France function on three levels:

(1) **tribunal de première instance** equivalent to magistrates' courts

(2) **tribunal de grande instance** equivalent to county courts

(3) **cour** higher courts such as:

— **cour d'appel** the court of appeal

— **cour d'assises**, equivalent to the Crown Court, sitting only at certain times of the year and dealing with the most serious offences (**crimes**)

— **cour de cassation** the court of final appeal, which is the equivalent of the Law Lords, where the judgements given by other courts are themselves judged

courrier (*nm*) in written work, the more common word for 'letter'. **j'accuse réception de votre courrier du 10 mars** I acknowledge receipt of your letter of 10 March

Courrier d'Entreprise à Distribution Exceptionnelle (CE-DEX) (*nm*) a form of business mail for organizations that receive a large daily volume of mail, which entitles them to special rates. *See below*

Courrier Individu(el) à Distribution Exceptionnelle (CIDEX) (*nm*) a form of special postal delivery in rural areas. *See above*

courrier poste restante (*nm*) *see* **poste restante**

cours (*nm*) a course. The term **cours** (or ⟨cycle⟩) is used in particular to refer to the different stages in primary education: **cours préparatoire**, for children aged 6 years; **cours élémentaire**, for those aged 7 to 9; **cours moyen**, for those aged 9 to 11. *See* **école élémentaire, école maternelle**

créancier/créancière (*nm/f*) a creditor

création d'une société (*nf*) the launch, or setting up, of a company

crèche (*nf*) a professionally run nursery for babies and toddlers, with a sliding scale of charges depending on income. It will often take care of children for the entire working day. **Garderie** is the more common term. *See also* **allocation, centre aéré, colonie de vacances, pouponnière, quotient familial**

crédit (*nm*) (1) credit   (2) a bank   (3) funds. **achat à crèdit/ vente à crédit** hire purchase, sale on easy terms. **crédit gratuit** interest-free credit. In France there is a seven-day cooling-off period (**délai de réflexion**) in which people who have signed a credit agreement are free to change their minds. **établissement de crédit** a lending or credit institution. **ouvrir un crédit** to take out credit

Crédit Agricole (*nm*) a national bank specializing in loans for agricultural purposes, but also offering mortgages

crédit bail (*nm*) leasing

crédit bancaire (*nm*) bank credit

crédit documentaire (*nm*) a written letter of credit

Crédit du Nord (*nm*) one of the largest national banks, with branches in most towns, whose controlling shareholder is the State

Crédit Foncier (*nm*) a bank specializing in loans for house-building

crédit hypothécaire (*nm*) a mortgage. *See* **aide personnalisée au logement, emprunt, hypothèque**

crédit immobilier (*nm*) a mortgage, a loan for house-buying. *See* **agence immobilière, hypothèque, prêt**

Crédit Lyonnais (*nm*) one of the largest national banks

crédit municipal (*nm*) a cross between a pawnbroker and a small finance house, offering loans on secured goods, plus a range of other financial services

Crédit Mutuel (*nm*) a large savings bank

créditeur (*nm*) a customer who is in credit. **Créditeur** is a false friend. A *creditor* is a **créancier**.

créer une société (*vb*) to set up a company

crime (nm) the third and most serious category of offence under French law, carrying punishments extending to imprisonment for life or (in theory at least) corporal and capital punishment. *See* **contravention, délit, infraction**

CRS *see* **Compagnies Républicaines de Sécurité**

cuisine équipée (nf) *see* **meublé**

cycle (nm) *see* **cours**

    cycle d'observation (nm) years one and two in a secondary school, covering the **classe de sixième** and the **classe de cinquième**. During this time children's abilities and aptitudes are monitored in order to determine which course of study they will follow. *See* **baccalauréat, brevet, collège, lycée**

    cycle d'orientation (nm) years three (**classe de quatrième**) and four (**classe de troisième**) in secondary school

DATAR *see* **Délégation à l'Aménagement du Territoire et à l'Action Régionale**

DDASS *see* **Direction Départementale de l'Action Sanitaire et Sociale**

DDCCRF *see* **Direction Départementale de la Concurrence, de la Consommation et de la Répression des Fraudes**

débats (nm.pl) proceedings, debates (in court)

débiteur/débitrice (nm/f) a debtor

débiteur/débitrice (adj) in debit, in debt, overdrawn, in the red. **compte débiteur** an account that is in the red

débouté (nm) non-suit. *See below*

déboutement (nm) non-suiting. *See below*

débouter (vb) to reject (usually in the sense of a list of claims made in court or to an official body). The formal decision of a court that the plaintiff has lost his or her case. To find against (the plaintiff). To non-suit

décès (nm) death, bereavement. **acte de décès** the final, official certificate issued by the **mairie** confirming the death and the completion of the necessary formalities. **certificat de décès** a death certificate issued by a doctor. **déclaration de décès** the act of reporting and registering a death at the town hall (**mairie**). *See* **déclaration de non-décès**

déclaration (nf) a declaration; a widely used term for a statement, registration, notification or attestation, usually in the form of writing or a certificate. Some of the more common types of **déclaration** are listed below:

déclaration de changement de domicile (nf) a notification of change of address

déclaration de faillite (nf) a declaration of bankruptcy

déclaration d'impôts (nf) a tax declaration, statement of earnings

déclaration de naissance (nf) a birth certificate. *See* **bulletin**

déclaration de non-condamnation (nf) a certificate or affidavit certifying that a person does not have a criminal record. *See* **casier**

déclaration de non-décès (nf) a declaration of non-death. The last word in bureaucracy, and an illustration of the emphasis the French place on the written word. This is an official certificate, which state officials may demand that you present while they are speaking to you face to face, which certifies that you are still alive and not in fact dead. Without it, they are legally entitled to deny that you are alive, which may lead to the failure to obtain various rights and entitlements. *See* **acte de notoriété**, **état civil**

déclaration de perte (nf) an official report of the loss or theft of an item, such as a passport, made out in a police station or other formal setting. An insurance company may demand this before paying out on a claim.

déclaration de ressources (*nf*) a statement of personal assets; a formal declaration giving an inventory of a person's wealth and possessions

déclaration de revenus (*nf*) a statement of income

déclaration en douane (*nf*) a customs declaration

déclaration préalable de construction (*nf*) planning permission for minor repairs, restoration or extensions, obtainable from the **mairie**. *See* **permis de construire**

dédit (*nm*) (1) a penalty, forfeit. **un dédit de cent francs** a hundred-franc penalty. *See* **amende, majoré, promesse de vente** (2) breach (of contract), breaking (of a promise), going back (on one's word)

déduction d'impôt au titre des immobilisations (*nf*) capital allowances

défaut (*nm*) (1) fault, lack (2) absence, failure to appear. **défaut de comparution** failure to attend. **faire défaut** to fail to turn up (following an order to attend). **jugement par défaut** judgement by default; a verdict awarded against someone who has failed to appear in court. *See* **comparution**

défenderesse (*adj*) relating to the defendant. **La partie défenderesse** may be used to describe the defendant or, more usually, the defendant's lawyer.

défendeur/défenderesse (*nm/f*) a defendant (in court), the person against whom a court action is brought

défense (la) (*nf*) counsel for the defence

défenseur (*nm*) counsel for the defence

déférer (*vb*) (1) to refer (a case to a different court or authority) (2) to hand over (an arrested person to a court)

dégrèvement (*nm*) tax relief, also known as **dégrèvement fiscal** or **dégrèvement d'impôt**

délai (*nm*) (false friend) not a delay, but a waiting period, deadline or interval. **dans un délai de dix jours** within ten days. **dépasser le délai** to exceed the time limit

délai-congé (*nm*) a period of notice (for leaving, or dismissal from, a post). *See* **licenciement**, **mise à pied**

délai de livraison (*nm*) a delivery time or period

délai de préavis (*nm*) *same as* **délai-congé**

délai de recouvrement (*nm*) the time limit for the recovery of a debt

délai de réflexion (*nm*) the seven-day cooling-off period, imposed by law on credit agreements, which allows buyers time to change their mind and pull out of a contract. *See* **démarchage**

délai de rigueur (*nm*) an absolute or final deadline

Délégation à l'Aménagement du Territoire et à l'Action Régionale (DATAR) (*nf*) the regional development board, one of whose roles is to encourage and advise foreigners thinking of setting up a business or investing in France. It produces a series of booklets covering grants, company law, tax, etc.

délégué/e de site (*nm/f*) an employee's representative in a small business – defined as one employing fewer than eleven people – which is working in unison with other businesses, for example, in a business park or an office block. *See* **délégué du personnel**

délégué/e des parents (*nm/f*) a parents' representative (on a school board, etc.)

délégué/e du personnel (*nm/f*) an employees' representative. Any business employing more than ten people must allow the workers to be represented in talks with the employer by delegates elected by the whole workforce. One of the roles of these delegates is to report complaints to the **Inspection du Travail**.

délégué(e)-élèves (*nm/f*) a pupils' representative (on a school committee)

délibéré (*nm*) deliberation, consultation. **mettre une affaire en délibéré** to give a court case over to a period of deliberation, as a prelude to reaching a judgement

délictueux/euse (*adj*) concerning the category of offences known as **délits**

délit (*nm*) a criminal offence of the second most serious type. *See* **infraction, voies de fait**

   délit de fuite (*nm*) failure to stop after a traffic accident

demande (*nf*) a request, application, claim. **faire une demande de qch** to apply for, make an application for something. *See* **chefs de la demande**

   demande d'aide judiciaire (*nf*) an application for legal aid. *See* **aide judiciaire, formuler**

   demande de convocation (*nf*) a formal request for someone to be brought before an official body (such as a court or Industrial Tribunal)

   demande d'emploi (*nf*) (1) the employment wanted, job-seeker section (in a newspaper) (2) a job application. **formuler une demande d'emploi** to apply for a job

   demande d'immatriculation au registre du commerce (*nf*) an application by a business for official registration

   demande en divorce (*nf*) a divorce petition

   demande en justice (*nf*) a formal request to a court to do something; a petition. **faire une demande** to make a request

   demande en renvoi (*nf*) a request for remittal: (1) a request to have a formal matter referred to a different authority for further consideration; (2) a request to have a case referred to a lower court; (3) a request for postponement (of a hearing, etc.)

   demande reconventionnelle (*nf*) a countersuit. Counter-charges, or a suit for damages, against someone who is suing you in court. This countercharge is often made as part of the defence. For example, the law on making false allegations is very strict, and someone sued is liable to demand damages if the case fails. *See* **atteintes à la vie privée, dénonciation calomnieuse, tierce opposition**

demandeur/demanderesse (*nm/f*) (1) a plaintiff, the person who brings the action (in a civil court), as opposed to the **défenseur**, the person *against* whom it is brought (2) an appellant, person bringing an appeal (in administrative matters, such as tax assessment)

démarchage (*nf*) door-to-door selling. There are restrictions on the type of business that can be conducted in this way, plus a mandatory cooling-off period during which the customer is free to back out of any agreement signed. It is illegal to sell door-to-door after 9 p.m. *See* **délai de réflexion, travail clandestin**

démarche (*nf*) a step, procedure or formality, usually in an administrative sense. **les démarches nécessaires** the necessary formalities

démembrement de propriété (*nm*) reduced property rights. For example, the right to live in a property until death, after which time the premises must revert to the original owner. *See* **cession-bail, copropriété, usufruit, viager**

déménagement (*nm*) house-moving. **prime de déménagement** a house-moving allowance or grant

demeure (*nf*) a residence, home. **à demeure** (*adv*) permanently. *See* **domicile, foyer**

démission (*nf*) resignation (from a post), handing in of notice

démissionner (*vb*) to resign, hand in one's notice. *See* **congé, préavis**

déni de justice (*nm*) denial of justice, professional misconduct. This is usually in the sense of a state official refusing to respect the rights of a member of the public, or of a judge refusing to hear a case. *See* **bavure, suspicion légitime, tribunal administratif**

dénonciation calomnieuse (*nf*) a libellous denunciation or malicious complaint. French laws on privacy are very strict, and discourage complaint. Anyone who makes an official complaint against another, to an authority such as the police or a state official, can be taken to court by the target of the complaint. The author then has to *prove* that the allegations are true. Failure to do so is a *criminal* offence under the **Code Pénal**, carrying a punishment of a fine or up to five years' imprisonment. *See* **atteintes à la vie privée, demande reconventionnelle**

déontologie (*nf*) professional ethics, rules of the profession

départ (*nm*) the mass exit from French cities at the beginning of holiday periods, which always results in huge traffic jams. *See* **rentrée**

département (*nm*) (1) one of 95 administrative divisions into which France is split. There are four additional overseas **départements**, Guyane, Guadeloupe, Martinique and Réunion. *See* **DOM/TOM** (2) a government ministry. *See* **code départemental** (*at* **départemental**)

Département d'Outre-Mer/Territoire d'Outre-Mer (DOM/TOM) (*nm*) In addition to the 95 departments of mainland France, there are four overseas departments: Guadeloupe, Guyane, Martinique and Réunion. Each of these is known as a **DOM (Département d'Outre-Mer)**. The term **TOM (Territoire d'Outre-Mer)** is used of other overseas territories less formally linked to the mainland, such as Saint-Pierre-et-Miquelon. *See above* and **hexagone**

départemental/e (*adj*) relating to a **département** (or county). **code départemental** a local or county law. **route départementale** a secondary road, a B road

dépendances (*nf.pl*) outbuildings (such as sheds or barns)

dépens (*nm*) (legal) costs. **être condamné aux dépens** to be ordered to pay costs. Note the difference between **dépens** and **dépenses**. *See also* **dommages et intérêts**

dépens en capital (*nm*) capital expenditure

dépenses (*nf.pl*) (1) outlay, cost, expenditure, expenses, fees (2) consumption (of gas, electricity, water, etc.)

dépenses scolaires (*nf.pl*) school expenses. A concept wider than that of school fees alone, which are **frais de scolarité**

déposer (*vb*) to lodge, file, deposit, put in (a request, etc.).

déposer une plainte contre qn to lodge a complaint against someone. **déposer les comptes** (vb) to file or draw up the accounts. **déposer une demande en recours** (vb) to lodge an application or appeal

déposition (nf) (1) depositing   (2) a deposition, testimony, formal statement. **faire une déposition** to make a deposition, to make a formal statement (to a court, etc.)

déposition mensongère (nf) perjury, false testimony. *See* **faux témoignage**

dépôt (nm) (1) a deposit   (2) a jail   (3) depositing   (4) a store, warehouse, depot. *See below*

dépôt de garantie (nm) a deposit, in the sense of a returnable one, particularly by a tenant when renting accommodation. The deposit is normally equivalent to two months' rent. It is common for tenants intending to leave to ask that the final two months' rent be taken from the deposit. *See* **caution**

dépôt de marchandise (nm) a goods depot, freight depot

dépôt d'ordures (nm) a rubbish tip, garbage dump

dépôt des comptes (nm) filing of accounts

dépôt de vente (nm) a second-hand shop selling goods on commission

député (nm) *see* **Assemblée Nationale**

dérogation (nf) a (special) dispensation, permission

désigné/e (adj) **personne désignée** (nf) a nominee, nominated representative. Someone authorized by another to carry out an act. *See* **pouvoir spécial de représentation**

désigner (vb) to nominate, appoint, name, designate, authorize

destinataire (nm) an addressee, the person to whom a letter is addressed. *See* **avis de réception**

destituer qn (vb) to dismiss someone, relieve them of a post or duties. *See* **licencier**

destitution (*nf*) dismissal, discharge (usually in an official or legal context). *See* **licenciement**

détention (*nf*) holding, detention, custody

> **détention préventive** (*nf*) custody. If they are not permanent residents in the country, foreigners under arrest in France, as in all European countries, may find difficulty in obtaining bail, as they have no fixed abode.

> **détention provisoire** (*nf*) remand, (pre-trial) custody. This can be of up to four months' duration. If after that time the accused is found innocent, compensation can be claimed.

DEUG *see* **Diplôme d'Etudes Universitaires Générales**

DEUST *See* **Diplôme d'Etudes Universitaires de Sciences et Techniques**

DGCCRF *see* **Direction Générale de la Concurrence, de la Consommation et de la Répression des Fraudes**

différend (*nm*) a dispute, disagreement, difference of opinion

Diplôme d'Etudes Supérieures Spécialisées (DESS) (*nm*) a vocational qualification awarded after one or two years of study after an MA or **maîtrise**. *See below*

Diplôme d'Etudes Universitaires de Sciences et Techniques (DEUST) (*nm*) a qualification inferior to a full degree (**licence**) awarded after two years at university, in scientific and technological subjects. *See below and* **premier cycle**

Diplôme d'Etudes Universitaires Générales (DEUG) (pronounced *durg*) (*nm*) *same as* **DEUST** above, but covering subjects other than science and technology. *See above and below*

Diplôme Universitaire de Technologie (DUT) (*nm*) a vocational qualification awarded after two years' post-school study in an **institut universitaire de technologie**. *See above*

direction (*nf*) (1) the management; a general term for the person or group of people in charge of a business or organization, e.g. manager, the management, post of manager, board of directors, editor, editorial board, headmaster   (2) the office (in a building) where any of the above are found (3) (in the Civil Service) the office or department of ... *See below*

Direction Départementale de l'Action Sanitaire et Sociale (DDASS) (*nf*) a branch of the social services giving financial and other help to people in extreme need. Among other things it handles the taking of children into care.

Direction Départementale de la Concurrence, de la Consommation et de la Répression des Fraudes (DDCCRF) (*nf*) a form of trading standards or consumer protection office, run by the State, which tries to ensure that laws aimed at protecting consumers are enforced. It is normally housed in the **cité administrative**. *See* **commission des clauses abusives, concurrence, dol**

Direction Départementale de l'Equipement (*nf*) the county office of supply, incorporating services like the water board. *See* **équipement, regard, service des eaux**

Direction Départementale du Travail et de l'Emploi (*nf*) *see* **ANPE, cité administrative, Inspection du Travail**

Direction du Trésor (*nf*) the Treasury department

Direction Générale de la Concurrence, de la Consommation et de la Répression des Fraudes (DGCCRF) (*nf*) the office of fair trading, a consumer complaints department. *See* **Agence Nationale pour l'Amélioration des Conditions d'Emploi, commission des clauses abusives, concurrence, Inspection du Travail**

directoire (*nm*) a management committee

dispensaire (*nm*) a local community clinic, health clinic

dispense (*nf*) (1) exemption (from national service, etc.) (2) special permission. *See below and* **autorisation**

dispense de bans (*nf*) marriage banns, announcement of a forthcoming marriage. For ten days preceding the ceremony, details of a proposed marriage must be displayed at the town hall where it will take place, and in the home towns of the couple. This allows objections to be raised, e.g. in the case of one of the pair being under age. *See* **communauté, émancipation, mairie, mariage**

disponibilité (*nf*) (1) availability   (2) (of a civil servant) leave of absence. *See* **mise en disponibilité**

disponible (*adj*) available. **disponible au travail** available for work. Strangely, in the case of a state official, **disponible** refers to someone who is not at work, but away on leave of absence. *See* **amplitude journalière, titulaire**

dispositif (*nm*) (1) a legal pronouncement   (2) the (third and final) part of a court decision which contains the actual court order, judgement or punishment, and which is introduced by the verb *décider*

disposition (*nf*) a clause or provision in a legal document. *See* **alinéa, avenant, engagement de non-concurrence**

dissoudre une société (*vb*) to wind up a company

district (*nm*) a group of **communes**, coming together to pool resources in transport, etc. *See* **agglomération, canton, communauté urbaine**

divorce (*nm*) divorce. *See* **communauté, juge aux affaires matrimoniales, pension alimentaire, prestation, séparation de corps**

doctorat (*nm*) a doctorate, roughly equivalent to a PhD. There are two kinds of **doctorat: doctorat d'état**, which takes around seven years to complete, and **doctorat de troisième cycle**, which takes three years.

document comptable (*nm*) a financial statement, accountant's report

documents-preuves (*nm.pl*) written or documentary evidence

dol (*nm*) fraudulent misrepresentation, deception (particularly in contracts). Any contract or agreement to which consent is obtained through misleading or withheld information, is invalid. This can refer to a formal contract like an offer of work, or to a private agreement like the selling of a second-hand car. *See* **nul, publicité mensongère, réticence, vices de consentement**

dolosif/ive (*adj*) fraudulent, deceitful. **manoeuvres dolosives** deception, trickery

domaine de l'Etat (*nm*) State-owned property or utilities

domaine public (*nm*) property in public, not private, ownership (e.g. roads, pathways, rivers)

domicile (*nm*) one's home, in the sense of principal or permanent address, as opposed to temporary residence (**résidence**). In a country strong on privacy, people enjoy the right not to be disturbed in their homes between the hours of 9 p.m. and 6 a.m., unless by a state official.

domicilier une société (*vb*) to domicile a company

dommages et intérêts (*nm.pl*) damages, financial compensation (in a court case)

DOM/TOM (*nm*) *see* **Département d'Outre-Mer/Territoire d'Outre-Mer**

donation (*nf*) a donation, gift. *See below and* **droits de donation**

> **donation entre époux** (*nf*) a 'gift between spouses'; a formal legally binding gift by one spouse to the other, while both are still alive. There is no English equivalent of this. Inheritance, the law of succession and wills operate in a completely different way to their British equivalents. In France, the children and parents of a deceased person, not the surviving spouse, inherit the estate. **Donation entre époux** is one way of offsetting this, but does not guarantee that the surviving spouse will automatically inherit the entire estate, in the way that making a formal will does. A difficult area easily misunderstood by foreigners, and requiring specialist legal advice. *See* **communauté, testament**

> **donation-partage** (*nf*) a type of will, certified by a **notaire**, detailing the division of the estate while the benefactor is still alive. *See* **acte authentique, testament**

dossier (*nm*) a dossier, file, case history. In civil cases the plaintiff and the defendant must disclose their arguments and evidence to each other before the hearing, as well as to the court. This is usually referred to as **la communication des dossiers**. *See* **communication, pièce**

dossier médical (*nm*) a patient's medical records. All patients have the legal right to inspect their own records.

double (*nm*) a copy, photocopy (of original document). *See* **copie certifiée conforme, expédition, notoriété**

droit (*nm*) (1) a right   (2) **droits** (pl) duty, tax. This is usually, but not always, in the plural. **exempt de droits** tax-free   (3) law. Examples of the different groups of meaning are listed under (1) to (3) below.

droit (1) (*nm*) a right

droit de chasse (*nm*) hunting rights. France being a large country with vast rural areas, hunting and shooting for game are widespread. Generally speaking, the owner of a property has rights to any game killed on it.

droit de grève (*nm*) the right to strike

droit de passage (*nm*) a right of access (to property). Right of access to a person, such as a child following a divorce, is **droit de visite**.

droits de reproduction (*nm.pl*) reproduction rights, licence to copy. *See* **contrefaçon**

droit de retrait (*nm*) the right of an employee to refuse temporarily, without incurring loss of pay, to undertake any work which he or she considers an actual or potential danger to life or health

droit de visite (*nm*) visiting rights, right of access (of divorced parents to their children, etc.). *See* **droit de passage**

droit de vote (*nm*) the right to vote; the vote

droit syndical (*nm*) the right to belong to a trade union, which is enjoyed by every worker

droits civils (*nm.pl*) civil rights

droits civiques (*nm.pl*) civic rights

droits dérivés (*nm.pl*) derived rights. These are rights that one person has by virtue of his or her relationship to someone else, for example, the rights of a wife or husband in regard to the spouse's insurance policy. *See* **pension de reversion**

droit/droits (2) (*nm.pl*) tax

droit de timbre (*nm*) stamp duty. Some official documents require payment of a small fee, which can be paid in the form of a stamp bought from a **tabac**. *See* **acte authentique**, **timbre**

droits de donation (*nm.pl*) gift tax

droits de douane (*nm.pl*) customs duty. *See* **accise**, **taxe**

droits d'enregistrement (*nm.pl*) a registration fee or duty, paid on some official forms. *See* **droit de timbre**

droits de mutation (*nm.pl*) transfer tax (shares)

droits de succession (*nm.pl*) inheritance tax, death duties

droit (3) (*nm*) law. *See* **code**, **tribunal** *and below*

droit civil (*nm*) civil law

droit commun (*nm*) common law, in the sense of those legal judgements not covered by specific courts or legislation. Common-law marriage in the English sense is **concubinage**.

droit constitutionnel (*nm*) constitutional law

droit de la famille (*nm*) family law

droit des affaires (*nm*) business law

droit des sociétés (*nm*) company law

droit fiscal (*nm*) fiscal law, tax law

droit international (*nm*) international law

droit pénal (*nm*) criminal law

droit privé (*nm*) private law, the law concerned with the individual

droit public (*nm*) public law, the law relating to the running and organization of the State

droit social (*nm*) labour and welfare law

durée (*nf*) duration, length, term, period (of a contract, etc.). *See* **contrat de travail à durée déterminée, contrat de travail à durée indéterminée, délai**

durée hebdomadaire maximum du travail (*nf*) the maximum length of the working week, which in France is 39 hours. *See below and* **amplitude journalière**

durée quotidienne maximum du travail (*nf*) the maximum length of the working day, which in France is 10 hours. *See above and* **amplitude journalière**

DUT *see* **Diplôme Universitaire de Technologie**

échéance (*nf*) (1) an expiry date (of work contract, etc.) (2) the date that a payment is due (of rent, etc.) (3) a maturity date (of an insurance policy, etc.) (4) (plural) payments owing, financial commitments. **le cas échéant** if the case arises. *See* **délai, durée**

échéancier (*nm*) a bill book

éclaireurs (*nm.pl*)/**éclaireuses** (*nf.pl*) Scout and Guide organizations. There are different types of Scouting organizations, some linked to churches, others independent. The main independent group is the **Eclaireuses et Eclaireurs de France**, the main Catholic Scouting body the **Scouts de France** (**Guides de France** for Girl Guides), and the main Jewish movement the **Eclaireuses et Eclaireurs Israélites de France**. *See* **Guides de France**

école (*nf*) a school, either for young children or for university-level high-flyers. *See below and* **collège, grande école**

école élémentaire (*nf*) the old name for a primary school. *See* **école maternelle, école primaire**

école libre (nf) a private school. *Also called* **école privée**

école maternelle (nf) a nursery school or playschool. Most French children attend state-run playschools before beginning primary education at the age of 6. The schools take children from the age of 2 upwards. Help and facilities for young children are exceptionally good in France. *See* **allocation, colonie de vacances, halte-garderie**

école normale (nf) a teacher training college. **Ecole Normale Supérieure (ENS)** a highly prestigious teacher training college for high-flyers. One of the **grandes écoles**

école primaire (nf) a primary school. *See* **école élémentaire**

école privée (nf) a private school. *Also called* **école libre**

Ecole Centrale de Lyon (nf) a national college that offers advanced courses in engineering. *See* **concours, grande école**

Ecole Centrale de Paris (nf) a privately owned institution offering advanced courses in engineering. *See* **concours, grande école**

Ecole Nationale d'Administration (ENA) (nf) one of the most prestigious of the **grandes écoles**, founded in 1945 for the training of an élite of administrators and civil servants. It recruits by highly competitive and heavily subscribed examination, attracting graduates from other **grandes écoles** and comparable institutions, as well as serving civil servants. Its graduates are called **énarques**. *See* **concours, grande école**

Ecole Nationale d'Ingénieurs (ENI) (nf) the national school of engineering, of which there are five centres. *See* **concours, ENSA, grande école**

Ecole Nationale d'Ingénieurs de Travaux Agricoles (ENITA) (nf) the national school of engineering for the agricultural industries, which also include food and horticulture. *See* **concours, ENSA, grande école**

Ecole Nationale Supérieure Agronomique (ENSA) (nf) the most prestigious of the national schools of agricultural and environmental engineering, which takes only the best of the successful candidates in the competitive examination. There are eight of these schools. *See* **concours, grande école**

Ecole Nationale Supérieure d'Arts et Métiers (ENSAM) (*nf*) the national school of industrial design. *See* **concours, grande école**

Ecole Nationale Supérieure des Arts Décoratifs (ENSAD) (*nf*) the national school of art and design, for those wishing to pursue careers in the decorative arts. *See* **concours, grande école**

Ecole Nationale Supérieure des Beaux-Arts (ENSBA) (*nf*) the national school of fine art, giving training in painting, sculpture and architecture. *See* **concours, grande école**

Ecole Polytechnique (*nf*) the most prestigious of the **grandes écoles**, recruiting school-leavers in what is recognized as the stiffest of all competitive examinations. Known as **X**, it has a reputation for producing the administrative and industrial élite. *See* **concours, grande école**

économique (*adj*) economic. **licenciement pour motif économique** (*nm*) redundancy, laying off, sacking of staff for economic reasons, i.e. on the grounds that the company is in financial difficulty. In French law, **motif économique** does not constitute **force majeure**, or *frustration of contract*, i.e. it is never automatically classed as circumstances beyond anyone's control that justify the laying off of staff without compensation. *See* **Conseil de Prud'hommes, licenciement**

écrit (*nm*) writing. **par écrit** in writing. The French normally insist on putting things in writing. Verbal contracts have little legal force and are highly unusual. No French person would dream of doing anything important on a verbal promise alone. *See* **contrat verbal, lettre recommandée**

écrou (*nm*) imprisonment, incarceration. **la levée d'écrou** release from prison

écrouer qn (*vb*) to imprison someone

EDF *see* **Electricité de France**

effectif (*nm*) the total number of (employees in a business, children in a school, etc.)

élaborer un texte (*vb*) to draft a text

élection (*nf*) an election. There are many different types of political election:

> **élections cantonales** (*nf.pl*) in which the **cantons** elect the member who will represent them on the **conseil général**

> **élections législatives** (*nf.pl*) election of **députés** to the **Assemblée Nationale**

> **élections municipales** (*nf.pl*) the electing by a **commune** of the local council (**conseil municipal**)

> **élection présidentielle** (*nf*) the once-every-seven-years election of the French president. *See* **septennat**

> **élections régionales** (*nf.pl*) the election of members of the **conseil régional**

> **élections sénatoriales** (*nf.pl*) the election of members of the **Sénat**

Electricité de France (EDF) (*nf*) the Electricity Board, which supplies all the electricity users in the country. Its offices are often twinned with the Gas Board (**Gaz de France**).

élu(e) (*nm/f*) an elected representative, usually in the context of local or regional government. *See* **conseiller**, **délégué**

émancipation (*nf*) (1) emancipation (2) a term applied to young people under the age of majority (**majorité**), which is 18, who wish to be counted for legal and administrative purposes as an independent adult, and not subject to parental control. This status of **mineur émancipé** is conferred in court – sometimes with, sometimes against, parental consent – usually in cases where the children have married or wish to live away from home.

émargement (*nm*) (1) annotating, marginal notes, adding written notes to a document (2) signature, initialling. **feuille d'émargement** (*nf*) an attendance register, payroll

émarger un document (*vb*) (1) to annotate a document or write

notes in the margin   (2) to sign a document by initialling it.
See **paraphe**

embaucher qn (*vb*) to hire someone

émettre des actions (*vb*) to issue shares

émettre un chèque (*vb*) to issue a cheque. *See* **chèque, compensable**

émettre un emprunt (*vb*) to grant a loan

émoluments (*nm.pl*) (solicitor's) fees, emoluments (as calculated on the professional scale). *See* **barème, frais, honoraires, notaire**

emplacement (*nm*) location. *See* **lieu de travail**

employé/e (*nm/f*) (1) an employee. **employé de banque** a bank clerk. **employé de bureau** an office worker. (2) more specifically, someone employed by the State with a status inferior to that of a **fonctionnaire**. *See* **agent titulaire, auxiliaire, contractuels**

emprise (*nf*) seizure or confiscation of goods by the authorities, sometimes following a court judgement, sometimes not. In the latter case, the victim can be eligible for compensation. Distinct from **astreinte**, which is the seizure of one private person's goods by another. *See* **déni de justice, saisie, sanction administrative**

emprunt (*nm*) (1) a loan   (2) the act of borrowing

emprunt-logement (*nm*) a mortgage, or loan for house or flat buying. Usually distinct from an **hypothèque**, which is reserved for second mortgages

emprunteur (*nm*) a borrower

en tant que (*prep*) as, in the capacity of, in one's position as. **je vous écris en tant que délégué du personnel** I write to you in my official capacity as employees' representative

ENA *see* **Ecole Nationale d'Administration**

énarque (*nm/f*) a graduate of the **Ecole Nationale d'Administration**, and so a member of a nationally recognized group of high-flyers, whose members fill over one-third of all top civil service posts. **Enarques** are required to work for the State for a minimum of ten years following graduation.

encontre (*prep*) **à l'encontre de qn** (of an official decision, etc.) against someone

encourir (*vb*) to incur, to be liable for. **encourir une peine** to incur a fine or punishment

endossement (*nm*) endorsement (of a cheque)

endosser un chèque (*vb*) to endorse a cheque

enfreindre (*vb*) to break, infringe. **enfreindre la loi** to break the law. *See* **délit**

engagement (*nm*) a formal, written promise, to do or not to do something. **engagements financiers** financial commitments or liabilities. *See below*

    engagement de non-concurrence (*nm*) a clause or condition attached to a work contract, in which the employee promises not to work for any of the employer's competitors. In practice this can mean anyone in the same line of business, apply up to a radius of 200 kilometres of the town in which they are to work, and cover not only the period in which they are in the new post, but for up to two years after leaving it. Signing such a document without legal advice can be very risky, as it may prevent someone from finding alternative employment in an entire region, *even if they are the victims of an unfair dismissal. See* **concours**, **équivalence**

engager une action (*vb*) to institute an action in court. *See* **entamer, poursuivre qn en justice, saisir la justice**

ENI *see* **Ecole Nationale d'Ingénieurs**

ENITA *see* **Ecole Nationale d'Ingénieurs de Travaux Agricoles**

énoncé (*nm*) a statement, the terms

énoncer (*vb*) to state, lay out, declare. **énoncer les faits** to make a formal statement, in the sense of a written account of events

enquête (*nf*) an inquiry, investigation. **mener une enquête** to conduct an inquiry

enregistrement (*nm*) (1) registration (2) the Registration Department. **frais d'enregistrement** registration fee, stamp duty (3) (in house-buying) stamp duty

enregistrer (*vb*) to register (a claim, etc.). *See* **lettre recommandée**

ENS *see* **Ecole Normale Supérieure**

ENSA *see* **Ecole Nationale Supérieure Agronomique**

ENSAD *see* **Ecole Nationale Supérieure des Arts Décoratifs**

ENSAM *see* **Ecole Nationale Supérieure d'Arts et Métiers**

ENSBA *see* **Ecole Nationale Supérieure des Beaux-Arts**

enseignement (*nm*) (1) education, in the sense of the educational system as a whole, or part of it (e.g. **enseignement primaire**, primary education) (2) the act of teaching (in a classroom) (3) teaching as a career

entamer (*vb*) to start, initiate. **entamer une procédure** to initiate proceedings

entretien (*nm*) (1) maintenance, upkeep (of a house, etc.) (2) keep (of a boarder) (3) an interview (4) a discussion. *See* **hébergement**

envoi contre remboursement (*nm*) a form of registered mail guaranteeing a certain level of compensation in case of loss. *See* **lettre recommandée**

envoi en valeur déclarée (*nm*) a more comprehensive form of registered mail, providing higher levels of insurance

équipement (*nm*) equipment, plant, fittings. **l'équipement électrique d'une maison** a house's electrical fittings. **équipement industriel** (industrial) plant. **Direction Départementale de l'Equipement** the council works department, *including* the water board. When you move into a new home, these are the people who have responsibility for connecting and disconnecting the water supply.

équivalence (*nf*) equivalence, comparability. **diplômes admis**

en équivalence recognized diplomas, degrees or qualifications awarded by foreign institutions such as universities, which are recognized by French employers and institutions as being as good as their French counterparts. One of the major difficulties of finding work in France is that foreign qualifications are often not recognized or are looked down upon. *See* **ANPE, concours, travail**

escroquerie (*nf*) fraud, a swindle. *See* **dol, dolosif, publicité mensongère**

ester en justice (*vb*) (1) to go to law   (2) to take part in a legal case

Etat (*nm*) the State. **agréé par l'Etat** government-approved, state-registered. *See* **Etatisme**

état civil (*nm*) civil status. A person's official status in France as defined by the register of births, deaths and marriages (**registre de l'état civil**). *See* **acte de notoriété, bureau de l'état civil, communauté, déclaration de non-décès, extrait d'acte de mariage, livret de famille**

état comptable (*nm*) a profit and loss account

état des lieux (*nm*) an inventory of fixtures (in a flat or house), taken at the start or end of a lease. In legal terms, Schedule of Condition (beginning), Schedule of Dilapidations (end). *See* **constat, huissier**

état futur d'achèvement (*nm*) the state of being in the process of construction, whether planned or actual. This concept is used in buying a house or flat 'on plan', when the contract of purchase is signed before the property has been built. *See* **contrat de réservation**

Etatisme (*nm*) state control; a political system in which the State – as opposed to the government or the people – plays a central role. One of the key differences between French and British society, and which everywhere influences character and behaviour, is the greater role of the State, particularly in regard to red tape, the stipulating of what can and cannot be done, and in laying down the correct way of carrying out procedures. *See* **système D**

étiquette (*nf*) a label, ticket. *See* **vignette**

étude (*nf*) (1) the office, practice (of a lawyer or a solicitor). *See* **avocat, cabinet, maître, notaire**. (2) study. **étude de marché** market research

éventuel (*adj*) possible. **éventuellement** (*adv*) possibly. Used often to convey 'perhaps'. A false friend. English *eventually* implies certainty, while the French **éventuellement** implies the opposite. **L'acquéreur éventuel** refers to a *potential* or *possible* buyer, not to 'the person who will eventually but definitely buy it'. A job offer that proposes **une période d'essai qui débouchera éventuellement en un poste permanent** means not 'a trial period that will lead *eventually* to a permanent post', but 'a trial period that *might, perhaps* lead' to one. *See* **dol, publicité mensongère**

examen médical prénuptial (*nm*) a marriage medical certificate. Those planning to marry must obtain a certificate from a doctor confirming their medical fitness to marry. This includes tests not only for venereal disease, but also for a range of other ailments and problems, including physiological incompatibility. *See* **communauté, mariage**

exceptionnellement (*adv*) in this particular instance, because of the exceptional circumstances. **par mesure exceptionnelle** as a special case. A false friend

exécuteur/trice (*nm/f*) an executor (of a will). *See* **administrateur, testament**

exécution (*nf*) (1) carrying out, execution, discharge (of a duty, etc.) (2) execution of a writ (against someone). **en exécution de la loi** in accordance with the law. *See* **juge de l'exécution**

exemplaire (*nm*) a copy, in the sense of a photocopy. **en deux exemplaires** in duplicate. *See* **ampliation, double, expédition, notoriété**

exonération d'impôt (*nf*) tax exemption

exonéré (*adj*) exempt (from). **être exonéré d'impôt** to be exempt from tax. *See* **franchise**

exonérer (*vb*) to exempt from

expédition (*nf*) a stamped and certified copy of an original document. *See* **ampliation, double, notoriété**

expert-comptable (*nm*) a (chartered) accountant

expert-foncier (*nm*) a surveyor (of buildings). The French generally use an architect to evaluate a property where the British would use a surveyor. A land surveyor is a **géomètre-expert.**

expertiser (*vb*) to value, evaluate (a property, etc.)

exploit d'ajournement (*nm*) a summons to appear. *See* **mise en accusation**

exploit d'huissier (*nm*) a writ, an official document served on someone by a court bailiff

exploitation (*nf*) working, running, operation (of a machine, etc.)

> **exploitation commerciale** (*nf*) a commercial concern, a commercial undertaking, a business

exposer (*vb*) (1) to exhibit, show, put on display (2) to explain, set out, air (grievances, etc.)

exposition (*nf*) (1) a display, exhibition (of goods) (2) an exposition, account (of events). **exposition des faits** a formal statement of events or of the circumstances surrounding a dispute. *See* **énoncer**

expropriation (*nf*) a form of compulsory purchase order. *See* **astreinte, emprise**

expulsion de domicile (*nf*) eviction

externe (*nm/f*) a term used in a variety of senses for an external or non-resident member of an institution. It might refer to a day-pupil in a boarding school as opposed to a boarder, a non-resident doctor in a hospital as opposed to a resident, or an external candidate in an exam as opposed to one from within the establishment or profession.

extrait d'acte de mariage (*nm*) a marriage certificate. *See* **régime matrimonial**

extrait de naissance (*nm*) *see* **bulletin de naissance**

F

facturation (*nf*) (1) invoicing, billing, invoice   (2) an invoice office

facture (*nf*) an invoice. *See* **bilan, bon,** etc.

facultatif/ive (*adj*) (1) optional, not compulsory (course, etc.)   (2) request (bus stop)   (3) discretionary (help). **aide facultative** *see* **aide légale**

faillite (*nf*) bankruptcy. **être en faillite** to be bankrupt. **faire faillite** to go bankrupt. **mettre qn en faillite** to make someone bankrupt. *See* **bilan, règlement judiciaire**

fait (*nm*) a fact *See* **voies de fait**

familial/e (*adj*) domestic, relating to the family. *See below*

famille nombreuse (*nf*) a large family. This is an official term referring to a family with three or more children. The French still have a problem in raising the birth rate, and continue to offer incentives to couples to have children. *See* **aide, allocation, carte nationale de priorité, congé de maternité, crèche, frais, livret de famille, quotient familial**

faux témoignage (*nm*) perjury, false evidence (in court). *See* **dénonciation calomnieuse, déposition mensongère, parjure**

fax (*nm*) *see* **télécopie**

Fédération de l'Education Nationale (FEN) (*nf*) a federation joining together the main unions representing teachers and lecturers

fédération d'industrie (*nf*) a federation grouping together unions representing workers within one industry

Fédération Nationale des Agents Immobiliers (FNAIM) (*nf*) the national federation of estate agents

FEN *see* **Fédération de l'Education Nationale**

férié (*adj*) **jour férié** (*nm*) a public holiday, official holiday, bank holiday. *See* **fête légale**

fermage (*nm*) (1) tenant farming (2) farm rent

fermeture annuelle (*nf*) the closure of a business for the annual holidays. *See* **départ, rentrée**

fête légale (*nf*) an official public or bank holiday (such as May Day). *See* **férié**

feuille (*nf*) a form, slip. *See* **bulletin, formulaire**

    feuille d'impôt (*nf*) a tax form

    feuille de maladie (*nf*) *same as* **feuille de soins**

    feuille de paie (*nf*) a pay slip, pay advice

    feuille de présence (*nf*) an attendance register, list of those present

    feuille de soins (*nf*) a medical form filled in by patients in order to claim back the cost of their medicines from Social Security. This is done by peeling off the special label (**vignette**) that comes on the boxes, and sticking it on to the form. The form is also called a **feuille de maladie**. Though medicine is expensive, most of the cost is refunded through medical insurance (**assurance maladie**). This form is not to be confused with the **ticket modérateur**, which is a form provided by the social services allowing free medical health care to certain types of people, such as the unemployed, expectant mothers or those with long-term illness.

fiche (*nf*) (1) a form, sheet, slip. (2) an index card. *See* **bon, bulletin, feuille, formulaire**

    fiche de paie (*nf*) a payslip, pay advice

    fiche de soins (*nf*) *same as* **feuille de soins**

fichier (*nm*) a file. *See* **casier**

filières (*nf.pl*) *see* **baccalauréat**

fisc (*nm*) the Inland Revenue; the taxman. **agent de fisc** a tax inspector. *See* **percepteur**

fixation (*nf*) fixing, setting (of a date, salary, etc.). **fixation du loyer** (*nf*) fixing of the rent

fixer (*vb*) to fix, set, arrange (date, fee, tax, etc.)

flagrant délit (*adv*) **en flagrant délit** red-handed, (caught) in the act of committing an offence. A private person has the right to make a citizen's arrest of someone caught in the act of committing a crime, but is liable to damages should the charge prove unfounded. *See* **atteintes à la vie privée, demande reconventionnelle, tribunaux des flagrants délits**

flags (*nm.pl*) *short for* **tribunaux des flagrants délits**

FNAIM *see* **Fédération Nationale des Agents Immobiliers**

FO *see* **Force Ouvrière**

foire à tout (*nf*) a kind of local fair or fête, taking over a whole town or quarter, and usually held once a year. It can vary enormously in size and content, and normally contains the equivalent of a car boot sale. However, it is unwise to treat the **foire à tout** as a car boot sale, as the French law on trading is very strict. A member of the public is allowed to participate in two **foires à tout** each year, and must first sign a declaration that this number has not been exceeded. Anyone exceeding this quota risks being classed as having a concealed occupation (**travail clandestin**) with all the tax problems this can bring. *See* **brocanteur**

foncier (*adj*) relating to land. **impôt foncier** land tax. **propriétaire-foncier** a landowner

fonction (*nf*) (1) duties, a post, office   (2) a function or role

   Fonction Publique (*nf*) the Civil Service

fonctionnaire (*nm/f*) a government employee, civil servant, State employee. This is a prestigious category, carrying many privileges and denoting someone who has passed a competitive examination (**concours**). Not to be confused with the humble **employé**. *See* **agent titulaire, auxiliaire, contractuels, vacation**

fondé (*nm*) **un fondé de pouvoir** an authorized representative, proxy. *See* **autorisation**

fonds (*nm*) (1) (in singular) a fund, collection   (2) (in plural) funds, sums of money. **fonds initial** capital outlay, start-up funds

fonds de commerce (*nm.sing*) a business, but in the sense of a lease or franchise. It refers to the *activity* rather than the *premises* in which the business takes place. It is common in the hotel, restaurant and café trade for owners to sell a business and allow someone else to run it and retain all the profit, while still retaining ownership of the premises for themselves. *See* **cession-bail**, **sous-bail**, **sous-traiter**, **rente viagère**

fonds de roulement (*nm.sing*) (1) working capital (2) running costs, emergency fund. In the case of a block of flats, this is a form of emergency fund contributed to by all the flat-owners, in addition to normal service charges (**cahier des charges**). It is used both for emergency repairs and for non-essential improvements to the building. *See* **conseil syndical**, **copropriété**

Fonds National de l'Aide au Logement (*nm.sing*) a fund that helps the young, the aged and the handicapped with grants towards housing costs

Fonds National de l'Emploi (*nm.sing*) a job-creation scheme that pays grants to enable unemployed people to seek work in other areas and employers to take on or retrain the unemployed or to keep on in part-time work employees they would otherwise have to make redundant. *See* **allocation spéciale mi-temps**

Fonds National de Solidarité (*nm.sing*) a fund that pays additional allowances to old people and the disabled

force (*nf*) force, strength. *See below*

force majeure (*nf*) forces beyond anyone's control; unforeseen or exceptional circumstances; exonerating circumstances. An argument that may be invoked by someone, such as an employer, who wishes to cancel a contract. *See* **économique**

force obligatoire (*nf*) legally binding force, that which is legally enforceable

Force Ouvrière (FO) (*nf*) a large, moderate union representing white-collar workers in the Civil Service and other professions

force publique (*nf*) the civil authorities, especially the police. **agent de la force publique** policeman or police-woman. **Force publique** is a more general term referring to the *authorities responsible* for the maintenance of public order, whereas **les forces de l'ordre** refers specifically to those like the police who *physically* enforce it.

forces de l'ordre (*nf.pl*) *see above*

forfait (*nm*) a fixed or set price. **travailler au forfait** to work for a flat rate or fixed amount

forfaitaire (*adj*) flat-rate, inclusive (price). **à prix forfaitaire** at an all-inclusive price. **amende forfaitaire** a fixed fine or penalty. **indemnité forfaitaire** an inclusive, or lump-sum, payment. *See* **majoré**

forfaiture (*nf*) an offence committed by a state official in the course of his duties, abuse of authority. *See* **bavure, tribunal administratif**

formation (*nf*) training, education, but usually in the sense of adult education, in-service training or other activity outside a formal school or university setting. *See below and* **enseignement, scolarisation**

formation complémentaire (*nf*) additional training

formation continue (*nf*) a broad term covering any form of training or education coming after formal education, which aims at improving the skills of employees. It covers in-service training and adult education. *See* **formation permanente**

formation permanente (*nf*) an alternative name for **formation continue**

formation professionnelle (*nf*) in-service training, courses of study for those already in work

former (*vb*) (1) to train, give professional training to. *See* **formation**   (2) **former un appel** to lodge an appeal. *See* **renvoi**

formulaire (*nm*) an (official) form. *See* **bon, bulletin, feuille, fiche**

formuler (*vb*) to draw up, formulate, set out. **formuler une demande** to make a formal request

fortune (*nf*) (1) wealth, capital, means. **avoir de la fortune** to have private means (2) (a) fortune. *See* **bien** (3) good fortune, good luck

fouille (*nf*) (1) a search (of person, house, etc.). *See* **perquisition** (2) an archaeological excavation

fournir des renseignements sur (*vb*) to give particulars or details about someone or something. *See* **coordonnées**

fourrière (*nf*) the police compound for towed-away vehicles. The French police are severe in this area. Cars not reclaimed within a short time are sold off or scrapped. In the case of old bangers, this period can be very short indeed.

foyer (*nm*) (1) a hostel or residence, for students, old people, foreign workers, the homeless, etc. (2) a home, domicile (especially for tax purposes). French tax laws are strict and may class a residence as someone's **foyer** for tax purposes, even though the owner seldom spends time there. *See* **coordonnées, demeure, domicile, impôt**

> **foyer des jeunes travailleurs** (*nm*) a type of YMCA, or cheap hostel for students and young workers

> **foyer fiscal** (*nm*) a tax home, the place to be counted as home for tax purposes

frais (*nm.pl*) fees, charges, expenses. *See below and* **droit(s)**, **émoluments, honoraires**

> **frais d'accouchement** (*nm.pl*) childbirth expenses

> **frais d'acte** (*nm.pl*) solicitor's fees, in the sense of the sum that relates to the drawing up of a specific document, rather than to the total amount owed for all the services given. *See* **barème, frais de notaire, honoraires**

> **frais de déplacement** (*nm.pl*) (1) travel expenses (incurred while performing work) (2) removal expenses (when moving to a new job)

> **frais d'enregistrement** (*nm.pl*) registration fees. *See* **radiation, timbre**

> **frais de notaire** (*nm.pl*) solicitor's fees, usually in the sense

of the *total* amount owed, which includes not only the **notaire**'s own charges (**frais d'acte**), but other charges such as stamp duty and Land Registry fees. Solicitor's fees in France can be heavy. The fee for handling the buying of a house may be as much as 15 per cent of the total price of the house, irrespective of the value of the property.

frais de scolarité (*nm.pl*) school fees. *See* **dépenses scolaires**

frais généraux (*nm.pl*) overheads, general running costs

France-Télécom (*nf*) the state-run telephone service. *See* **minitel, PTT**

franchise (*nf*) (1) franchising. *See* **fonds de commerce** (2) (in insurance) excess, the amount that falls outside the minimum value of a claim, for example, when the insured person has to pay the first £50 of any claim on a car insurance (3) exemption. **en franchise** duty-free. **franchise douanière** exemption from customs duty. **franchise postale** official-paid (letter), prepaid envelope

franchisé (*nm*) a franchisee, someone who has taken out a franchise

franchiseur (*nm*) a franchiser, someone who gives a franchise

frappé (*adj*) **être frappé de** to be subject to. *See below*

frapper (*vb*) to impose, hit, make something subject to. **frapper qn d'une amende** to impose a fine on someone. **un jugement frappé d'appel** a judgement against which an appeal has been lodged. *See* **contradictoire, ressort**

fraude (*nf*) fraud, evasion. **fraude fiscale** tax evasion. *See* **dol, publicité mensongère**

Front National (*nm*) an extreme right-wing political organization, associated with the name of Jean-Marie Le Pen, controversial for its policies on race and immigrants

gain de cause (nm) a win, success (in a court case). *See* **ressort**

garant/e (nm/f) (1) a guarantor, someone who guarantees something, vouches for someone, or promises that something will happen (2) a guarantee, in the legal sense of offering security for someone or something, rather than in the commercial sense of a piece of paper given with something bought in a shop. **se porter garant pour qn, se servir de garant à qn** to stand bail for someone. *See* **attestation, caution, garantie, répondant**

garantie (nf) a guarantee (given with an item bought in a shop, etc.). *See* **caution, garant, non-garantie**

    garantie décennale (nf) a ten-year guarantee, given with a newly constructed house or flat

    garantie de parfait achèvement (nf) a one-year, making-good guarantee, which can be taken out on newly built property, and which promises to put right any defects discovered during the first year

    garantie légale (nf) a statutory guarantee, legal guarantee. Any item sold in France is guaranteed by law against any fault which makes it unfit for the purpose for which it was sold, provided that the fault was not caused by the purchaser and was not readily apparent in the object at the time it was sold.

garde à vue (nf) taking in for questioning. The French police have the right to take in any adult for questioning and observation for a period of twenty-four hours, without having to bring charges or present a warrant. During this period a body search can be carried out, and the detainee is not allowed to consult a lawyer. *See* **détention provisoire, interpellation, prévention**

garde champêtre (nf) a type of local policeman who undertakes minor duties, such as accompanying the school bus (**ramassage scolaire**) and acting as school crossing patrol

Garde Républicaine (*nf*) a police unit, part of the **Gendarmerie Nationale**, which carries out ceremonial duties such as state escorts and mounting guard on major public buildings

garderie *see* **halte-garderie**

gardien/gardienne (*nm/f*) the more common word for a **concierge**, the caretaker-cum-receptionist of an apartment block

gardien de la paix (*nm*) an ordinary policeman of the **police municipale**

Gaz de France (GDF) (*nm*) the state-run gas company

gendarme (*nm*) a type of uniformed policeman, belonging to the **gendarmerie**. *See below and* **Compagnies Républicaines de Sécurité, garde champêtre, officier de paix, police**

> **Gendarmerie Nationale** (*nf*) one of the uniformed branches of the French police force, officially part of the Ministry of Defence and normally housed in barracks attached to the police station. Young men were able to opt to do their national service (**service national**) in this unit.

géomètre-expert (*nm*) a surveyor. The French concept of a surveyor is different from the British. *See* **expert-foncier**

gérant (*nm*) a manager. **gérant d'immeuble** a managing agent (of a block of flats, etc.). *See* **conseil syndical, direction**

gîte (*nm*) a holiday home, either purpose-built or converted from a farmhouse. Some are run privately, others by the local authorities. Some are open for long-term lets at reduced prices during the winter months.

grande école (*nf*) The **grandes écoles** are a group of higher education establishments that take only the best students and enjoy an unrivalled reputation for academic excellence, prestige and producing the nation's élite. Entry is by competitive examinations. *See* **concours** *and individual entries under* **Ecole**

grand(e) invalide civil(e) (*nm/f*) a category of severely disabled people entitled to a range of grants and concessions, including disabled car stickers. *See* **aide, allocation, carte, pension**

grand(e) invalide de guerre (*nm/f*) a disabled ex-serviceman or -woman. *See* **mutilé de (la) guerre**

greffe (*nf*) the office of clerk of the court (**greffier**)

greffier (*nm*) the clerk or registrar of the court or industrial tribunal, to whom all queries concerned with a given case should be addressed. The **greffier** will advise on tribunal procedure, but does not give out general information on points of law. For that you need to consult a lawyer, the **maison de l'avocat** or the **Inspection du Travail**. *See* **arbitrage, avocat**

grève (*nf*) a strike, industrial action. **faire la grève** to be on strike. *See* **arrêt de travail**

grief (*nm*) a grievance, grounds for complaint. **acte faisant grief** a decision or act of the authorities which a member of the public feels is unjustified or gives grounds for complaint. *See* **bavure**

groupe hospitalier (*nm*) *see* **centre hospitalier**

guichet (*nm*) (1) a ticket office (2) a booking office (3) a counter (in a bank, etc.) (4) a window (where payment is made or queries dealt with) (5) a hatch (in a wall, etc.). **guichet automatique de banque** a cash machine (at a bank)

Guides de France (*f.pl*) a leading Guides organization, linked to the Catholic Church. *See* **eclaireurs/eclaireuses**

halte-garderie (*nf*) *same as* **garderie**, a nursery or playschool for children under 6. *See* **crèche, école maternelle**

handicapé/e (*nm/f*) a handicapped person. **handicapé mental** a mentally handicapped person. **handicapé physique** a physically handicapped person. *See* **allocation, carte d'invalidité, invalide, pension**

harcèlement sexuel (*nm*) sexual harassment

haute assemblée (*nf*) an alternative name for the **Sénat**

hébergement (*nm*) lodging, putting up, board and lodging. *See* **location**

heures creuses (*nf.pl*) off-peak hours

heures supplémentaires (*nf.pl*) overtime

hexagone (*nm*) a popular term for European mainland France, as distinct from the whole of France's territorial possessions including its colonies. Derives from the roughly six-sided shape of the country. *See* **Département d'Outre-Mer/Territoire d'Outre-Mer**

honoraires (*nm.pl*) fees (of a professional person such as a lawyer). In the case of the legal profession, the term normally refers to fees *not* calculated by a fixed scale. *See* **barème, charges, frais, note**

hôpital (*nm*) a hospital. **hôpital conventionné** a National Health hospital. *See* **centre hospitalier, clinique, dispensaire**

hors taxe (*adj*) duty-free. *See* **franchise**

hospitalier/ière (*adj*) relating to a hospital. *See* **centre, groupe**

hôtel (*nm*) (1) a hotel   (2) a general term used in the title of various public buildings. *See below*

   hôtel de police (*nm*) a police station

   hôtel des ventes (*nm*) auction rooms, auctioneers

   hôtel de ville (*nm*) a town hall

   hôtel du département (*nm*) a county hall, the main office of the county services, where, among other things, the **conseil général** meets

huissier (huissier de justice) (*nm*) a type of bailiff who carries out official tasks such as serving summonses, and who can be hired by anyone wanting to ensure something is done in an above-board fashion – such as making inventories in flats. The **huissier** also acts as an usher in court or ministry buildings. *See* **constat, exploit d'huissier**

hypothèque (*nf*) a second mortgage, secured by a property. *See* **crédit, emprunt-logement, prêt conventionné, prêt patronal**

I

Ile de France (*nf*) the region immediately surrounding Paris, which includes several **départements** and contains almost 20 per cent of the population of France. Sometimes known as the **région parisienne**, it has its own **conseil régional**.

l'Ilot (*nm*) a voluntary organization providing support for the underprivileged, former prisoners and the homeless

immatriculation (*nf*) one's social security number (without which no benefits can be paid). **plaque d'immatriculation** a car number plate

immatriculé/e (*nm/f*) a registered person, someone who has filled in the appropriate forms. *See* **administré, radiation**

immatriculer (*vb*) to register or formally take down the particulars of someone. *See* **radiation**

immeuble classé (*nm*) a listed building. *See* **certificat d'urbanisme, plan d'occupation des sols, servitudes**

immobilier/ère (*adj*) *see* **agence immobilière**

important/e (*adj*) a false friend, which means *large*, not *important*. **des frais importants** heavy costs, not simply charges that it is important not to forget to pay

imposition (*nf*) taxation. **avis d'imposition** a tax bill, tax reminder

impôt (*nm*) a tax, duty. *See* **accise, tarif, taxe**

  impôt de solidarité sur la fortune (*nm*) a type of wealth tax

  impôt local (*nm*) local authority taxes. *See* **taxe**

  impôt sur le revenu (*nm*) income tax

inculpé/e (*nm/f*) the accused. *See* **accusé, coupable, prévenu, responsable**

indemnité (*nf*) compensation, allowance. *See* **allocation, avantages**

indemnité d'immobilisation (*nf*) a holding deposit in property buying, which reserves a property exclusively for the person paying the deposit. The seller cannot withdraw from the sale without incurring financial penalties. *See* **contrat de réservation, promesse bilatérale, provision**

indemnité de logement (*nf*) housing allowance. *See* **aide personnalisée au logement**

indemnité de préavis (*nf*) compensation for dismissal without proper notice

indemnité de transport (*nf*) travel allowance. *See* **frais de déplacement**

indemnité forfaitaire (*nf*) *see* **forfaitaire**

Indicateur Qualitel (*nm*) a directory of newly built properties guaranteeing the standards used in their construction

infraction (*nf*) an offence, breach of the law. There are three types and levels of offence, which in ascending order of seriousness are:

(1) **contravention** (*nf*) a petty offence punishable by a fine, e.g. speeding. These are dealt with in the local **tribunal d'instance civile** or **tribunal de police**. There are a number of other **tribunaux** at this level, known collectively as **tribunaux d'exception**.

(2) **délit** (*nm*) an offence for which the punishment is greater than two months' imprisonment or a fine of 12,000 francs

(3) **crime** (*nm*) the most serious category of crime carrying corporal or capital punishment or imprisonment for life

(4) Note also **quasi-délit** (*nm*), or negligence, where personal injury or damage is caused without intention on the part of the person responsible. *See* **amende, cour, tribunal**

injonction de payer (*nf*) an injunction allowing the recovery of money unpaid on a written agreement. In this simplified procedure, the creditor is normally granted automatic right to recovery. *See* **astreinte**

inscription scolaire (*nf*) putting a child's name down for a place in a school. This is normally done at the town hall, and requires the production of a variety of legal and medical documents. *See* **certificat de scolarité, école maternelle, livret de famille, quotient familial**

inspecteur du travail (*nm*) a work inspector, charged with ensuring that employers and workers obey the labour law (*see* **Code du Travail**). Their office is in the **cité administrative**, and their services and advice are free. They can be used by any employee experiencing difficulties with an employer. *See* **conciliation, Conseil de Prud'hommes, contrat de travail, licenciement**

Inspection du Travail (*nf*) the office of the work or factory inspectors. *See* **inspecteur du travail**

instance (*nf*) (1) legal proceedings. **introduire une instance** to initiate proceedings. (2) authority. **en instance** pending (of divorce, etc.), being held (of a parcel or letter), in the process of happening. **en première instance** following the judgement of a preliminary court. **en seconde/deuxième instance** following appeal (to a higher court). *See* **cour, tribunal de grande instance**

instituteur/institutrice (*nm/f*) an obsolescent term for a teacher in a primary school. *See* **école maternelle, école primaire**

interdiction de séjour (*nf*) a banning order imposed by a court, preventing someone from living in a specified area for a period of up to ten years

intérimaire (*nm/f*) a temporary worker or stand-in. What in English is called a 'temporary post' is covered in French by three different concepts, *durée déterminée*, *intérimaire*, and *temporaire*. *See below and* **contrat de travail, travail intermittent, vacation**

intérimaire (*adj*) interim, temporary, stand-in. **poste intérimaire** temporary cover for an absent employee. This term is used specifically about one of the limited number of grounds on which a French employer can take on a temporary worker on a fixed-term contract. A 'temp' in the British sense of someone working for a temping agency is un *employé temporaire*. An employee who is temporary in the sense of being on a fixed-term contract is working with a **contrat de travail à durée déterminée**. *See* **contrat de travail à durée indéterminée, motif de l'appel, requalification**

internat (*nm*) (1) a boarding-school, dormitory in a school (2) boarding (3) a period of training within an establishment (such as that of a houseman in a hospital). *See* **formation**

interne (*nm/f, adj*) a general term describing a person or procedure operating within an establishment, such as a boarder in a boarding-school, a houseman in a hospital, or promotion exams. *See* **externe**

interpellation (*nf*) calling in for questioning by the police. *See* **avis, comparution, convocation, garde à vue, mandat**

interpeller (*vb*) to call in for questioning

invalide (*nm/f*) a disabled person. *See* **handicapé**. A **grand invalide civil** refers to a person who has lost the use of one or both legs, who is blind or whose mental disabilities require the presence of a helper. People in this category are entitled to a special car sticker plus a number of other benefits. *See* **allocation, carte d'invalidité, carte station debout pénible, pension**

invalidité (*nf*) disablement, disability

irrégulier/ère (*adj*) irregular, not in order. **vous êtes en situation irrégulière** your papers are not in order

irrépétible (*adj*) one-off. **Les frais irrépétibles** are expenses incurred in the process of bringing a court case, but not part of a wider claim for damages, which the winner of the case may ask the court to award in costs. *See* **demande reconventionnelle, dépens, dommages et intérêts**

J

jour de congé (*nm*) a day off (work)

jour de fête (*nm*) a feast day, commemorative day, public holiday

jour férié (*nm*) a public or bank holiday

jour ouvrable (*nm*) a weekday, workday

juge (*nm*) a judge. As in everything, French law is administered in a specialized and compartmentalized way. Judges are normally specialists in one of the fields listed below. *See* **magistrat**

> **juge aux affaires familiales** (*nm*) a judge specializing in family law and divorce. Until 1994 known as a **juge des affaires matrimoniales**

> **juge-commissaire** (*nm*) a judge made responsible for seeing that a difficult part of a wider legal procedure is carried out

> **juge consulaire** (*nm*) a judge who sits in a **tribunal de commerce**

> **juge de l'application des peines** (*nm*) a judge in a **tribunal de grande instance** who has responsibility for ensuring that the punishments handed down by a court are carried out. It is this judge who would have responsibility for areas such as reducing sentences for good behaviour, or checking that the conditions of suspended sentences are being obeyed. This role is similar to that of the **juge de l'exécution**, the difference being that the former is concerned with the practical implementing of a sentence, while the latter focuses on secondary legal problems that might arise.

> **juge de l'exécution** (*nm*) the judge in a **tribunal de grande instance** responsible for any legal problems that arise as a result of a judgement handed down by a court. *See above*

> **juge de l'expropriation** (*nm*) a judge in a **tribunal de grande instance** who fixes the amount of compensation in a compulsory purchase order (**expropriation**)

juge d'instruction (*nm*) an examining magistrate. The **juge d'instruction** marks a key difference between the British and French systems of justice. In France, someone accused of a crime is summoned to appear before an examining magistrate, whose task is to investigate the complaint, gather evidence and then decide whether the matter should be taken before a court. Sometimes known as a **magistrat instructeur**. In more difficult cases this judge is assisted by a **juge de la mise en état**. *See* **juge rapporteur**

juge de la mise en état (*nm*) a judge who works alongside a **juge d'instruction** in more complex cases, and who has responsibility for preparing the ground for the hearing proper, such as by ensuring that all due formalities – like the exchange of dossiers – are completed. *See* **communication de pièces**

juge des affaires matrimoniales (*nm*) *see* **juge aux affaires familiales**

juge des enfants (*nm*) a judge in a juvenile court

juge des loyers (*nm*) a judge in the equivalent of a rent tribunal, responsible for dealing with disputes between private landlords and tenants. *See below and* **bail**, **loi de 1948**, **loi Méhaignerie**, **maintien dans les lieux**

juge des loyers commerciaux (*nm*) a judge who rules on disputes over commercial rents. *See above and* **fonds de commerce**

juge des référés (*nm*) a judge called upon to make an emergency ruling at short notice. Though such a ruling is provisional, it has immediate effect. Such a judge can belong to any of the specialist divisions of the courts.

juge des tutelles (*nm*) a judge who gives rulings in matters relating to the guardianship of children

juge rapporteur (*nm*) a judge who, in complex cases, makes a report (**rapport**) in order to clarify and simplify issues relating to the hearing of the case proper. This preliminary stage is part of the process of **mise en état** and is supervised by a **juge de la mise en état** or **conseiller de la mise en état**.

juge unique (*nm*) a judge who takes charge of a case alone, rather than as part of a panel. Found mainly in the lower courts

jugement (*nm*) (1) a verdict, decision, judgement (in a court) (2) a sentence. *See* **bureau de jugement**

juré/jurée (*nm/f*) a juror, someone sitting on a jury

juridiction (*nf*) (1) jurisdiction, competence **(compétence)** (2) an alternative word for a court or a group of courts of the same type, e.g. **la juridiction prud'hommale** matters covered by the industrial tribunal **(Conseil de Prud'hommes)**. *See* **compétence**

juridictions de droit commun (*nf.pl*) *see* **droit commun**

juridictions d'exception (*nf.pl*) an alternative name for the specialized courts or **tribunaux d'exception**

jurisconsulte (*nm*) a legal expert able to give advice on points of law. *See* **avocat, avoué, conciliation**

jury (*nm*) a jury. French juries have nine members. There are never juries in *civil* cases in France.

justice (*nf*) justice, law. *See* **aller en justice, ester en justice, saisir la justice**

justiciable (*adj*) subject to court action

justiciable (*nm/f*) the accused, the person to be brought to court. *See* **accusé, inculpé**

ledit/ladite (*adj*) aforementioned. *See* **sur-cité**

légitime défense (*nf*) (legitimate) self-defence

lettre recommandée (*nf*) a recorded letter. Recorded letters are a way of life in France, and are used far more commonly than in Britain. No French person would dream of sending a vital letter or document other than by **lettre recommandée avec avis**

de réception, i.e. by a recorded letter containing a proof of delivery coupon, which is signed by the receiver and returned by the post office to the sender.

levée (*nf*) (1) collection (of post) (2) the closing (of a hearing, etc.) (3) the lifting (of a punishment) (4) the levying, raising (of a tax). *See* **ampliation, écrou**

levée de jugement (*nf*) a transcript or copy of a court judgement. *See* **ampliation**

libération conditionnelle (*nf*) parole. The conditional release of prisoners for good behaviour before the full term of their imprisonment is served

liberté d'aller et venir (*nf*) a right of access, freedom of movement. *See* **droit de passage, droit de visite**

liberté surveillée (*nf*) probation

licence (*nf*) (1) a degree awarded after three years' study in higher education; the equivalent of a BA or BSc (2) a permit, licence. *See* **autorisation, diplôme, maîtrise, permis**

licencié/e (*n/mf*) a graduate. **professeur licencié** a graduate teacher

licenciement (*nm*) dismissal, sacking (from employment). **licenciement abusif** aggravated dismissal, an unfair dismissal carried out in a particularly offensive manner, without respect for proper procedure. **licenciement pour motif économique** redundancy, lay-off for economic reasons. **licenciement sans cause réelle ou sérieuse** unfair dismissal. *See* **Conseil de Prud'hommes, force majeure, Inspection du Travail, rétrogradation**

licencier (*vb*) to sack, dismiss

lieu de travail (*nm*) a place of work. Though the place of work must be stipulated on the work contract, small print in the wording may allow the employer to force the employee to work in a different town, a different part of the country, or a series of different towns or parts of the country, to those promised. This can make house-buying or the education of children difficult. *See* **contrat de travail, convention collective, dol, publicité mensongère**

lire (*vb*) to read. **dans l'attente de vous lire** (in letter-writing) in the expectation of receiving a prompt response

liste électorale (*nf*) an electoral register, list of those eligible to vote

litige (*nm*) litigation, a lawsuit. *See* **affaire, contentieux, justice**

livret de famille (*nm*) a family registration book. This is a book issued by the town hall (**mairie**) to couples when they marry, or to the unmarried parents of newly born children. It contains the details of both parents, and spaces for the details of the birth and death of future children. It must be presented when applying for certain benefits and is a useful red-tape cutter generally.

locataire (*nm*) a tenant, the person to whom a property is rented. *See* **propriétaire**

location (*nf*) renting, leasing (of property, etc.). **contrat de location** a lease. *See* **bail, caution, cession-bail, dépôt de garantie, juge des loyers, sous-location**

logement social (*nm*) subsidized housing. *See* **aide personnalisée au logement**

loi (*nf*) law, or Act of Parliament

> **loi de 1948** (*nf*) an important law for tenants, offering protection against excessive rent-hikes

> **loi Méhaignerie** (*nf*) a law protecting cohabiting tenants and dependants from the consequences of divorce, separation or bereavement. It guarantees the right of a person who is the partner or dependant of someone in whose name a property is rented to continue as the official tenant of the property if that person dies or moves out. *See* **maintien dans les lieux**

> **loi Scrivener** (*nf*) a law which protects the rights of the borrower against exploitation by those selling, or arranging loans on, a property

lot (*nm*) (1) a prize (in the national lottery) (2) a plot (of land) (3) a batch, lot, consignment (of goods). *See below and* **terrain**

lotir (*vb*) (1) to divide up a piece of land into (building) plots (2) to offer for sale in lots (3) to divide up and share out (a will, etc.)

lotissement (*nm*) (1) a building estate offering individual building plots for sale (2) a housing development or estate. Note that the law relating to **lotissements** is different in important respects from that covering its British equivalent. *See* **viabilisé**

loto (*nm*) the national lottery

lu et approuvé (*adj*) read and approved. In addition to signing their name to a document, people are often required to write these words beneath their signature. *See* **paraphe**

lycée (*nm*) a secondary school, roughly equivalent to a sixth-form college, preparing children for their **baccalauréat** exams. It is one of the four stages of children's education – **école maternelle**, **école primaire**, **collège**, **lycée**. The **lycée** accepts children from the age of 15, after they have left their 11–15 age group **collège**. *See* **proviseur**. **Lycée** is a general term for a 15 + school, but covers a number of specialist institutions such as: **lycée agricole**, specializing in agricultural science; **lycée d'enseignement professionnel**, offering vocational courses and specific **baccalauréat** options; **lycée d'enseignement technologique**, specializing in technical subjects; and **lycée international**, taking a high proportion of foreign students and usually offering the international baccalaureate (**baccalauréat international**).

magistère (*nm*) a prestigious, high-level postgraduate degree, awarded after three years of study. *See* **doctorat**, **licence**, **maîtrise**, **mastère**

magistrat (*nm*) a judge, magistrate. There are two types of **magistrat**. The first category is the **magistrat debout** or

magistrat du parquet, literally, 'standing magistrate' or 'floor magistrate'. These magistrates are part of the office of the State Prosecutor (**Procureur de la République**). The second category is the **magistrat assis** or **magistrat du siège**, literally, 'sitting magistrate'. This is the normal seated court judge, or the 'bench'.

magistrat instructeur (*nm*) *same as* **juge d'instruction**

maintien dans les lieux (*nm*) a right of abode. The right of a person and his or her dependants, who are already living in a rented property, to remain there after the death, divorce or abandonment of their partner, even if the departed person alone was named on the letting contract. Such remaining tenants may be evicted only if the property is to be occupied by the owner or the owner's family, or if it is to be demolished, and if replacement accommodation is provided which is of a standard at least equal to that of the existing home. This applies always in the case of people aged 70 or over, or in the case of people on very low incomes. *See* **conjoint, loi Méhaignerie**

maire (*nm*) a mayor. The **maire** is the head of the local council (**conseil municipal**) and the borough, which is normally a **commune** in country areas and an **arrondissement** in a city. The post is practical rather than ceremonial, with French mayors carrying out more of the duties of an ordinary state official, such as marriages and other civil formalities, than would be the case with their British counterparts.

maire-adjoint (*nm*) an assistant mayor. There may be several of these.

mairie (*nf*) a town hall, sometimes called **hôtel de ville**

maison (*nf*) (1) a house, home (2) a general term for an official building. *See below*

maison centrale (*nf*) a prison, for long-term stay

maison d'arrêt (*nf*) a prison, for short-term offenders. *See also* **maison de correction**

maison de correction (*nf*) a prison, for short-term offenders

maison de l'avocat (*nf*) a kind of (fee-charging) citizens' advice bureau or cut-price law centre, where people can get preliminary advice on legal problems. The cost of the service can vary considerably. The address is available from the **palais de justice** or **Conseil de Prud'hommes**.

maison de la culture (*nf*) an arts centre

maison de retraite (*nf*) a retirement home

maison des jeunes et de la culture (*nf*) a form of youth club, or youth and community centre, offering sports and cultural activities. *See* **centre de loisirs**

maison maternelle (*nf*) a hostel for pregnant women or new mothers. *See* **allocation**, **crèche**

maître (*nm*) a term of address for a lawyer or solicitor. Written **Me.** in correspondence. *See* **avocat**, **notaire**

maître auxiliaire (*nm*) an auxiliary teacher, on a lower scale of pay and with fewer employment rights than a fully qualified one. Generally speaking, these are the only posts open to foreigners in French state schools. *See* **concours**, **équivalence**, **professeur**

maître de conférences (*nm*) a university lecturer

maîtrise (*nf*) the equivalent of a master's degree (MA)

majeur/e (*nm/f*) someone who has reached the age of majority; an adult. *See below*

majoration (*nf*) (1) a rise, increase (in a bill) (2) an overestimate (3) a surcharge, financial penalty

majoré/e (*adj*) increased, subject to a surcharge or financial penalty. *See* **amende**, **forfaitaire**

majorer (*vb*) (1) to increase, put up (salary, price, etc.) (2) to put a surcharge or penalty on. *See* **amende**

majorité (*nf*) age of majority, coming of age, adulthood (at age 18 in France). It is possible for young people to be legally classed as adults before this age, if they apply for **émancipation**.

mandat (*nm*) (1) a money order, postal order (2) a (police) warrant (3) power of attorney, proxy, authorization (4) a mandate

mandat-carte (*nm*) a money order, authorizing the doorstep delivery of cash to the payee

mandat d'amener (*nm*) a summons. *See* **convocation**, **interpellation**

mandat d'arrêt (*nm*) an arrest warrant

mandat de comparution (*nm*) a subpoena, summons (of a witness) to appear before an official body. *See* **avis**, **comparaître**, **convocation**, **mise en accusation**

mandat de dépôt (*nm*) a committal order, an official order sending someone to jail. *See* **dépôt**, **maison**

mandat de perquisition (*nm*) a search warrant. *See* **fouille**

mandat exclusif (*nm*) sole agency; a written authorization given by the seller of a property to an estate agency, allowing it to act as sole agent. In return a discount on fees is obtained. *See* **mandat simple**

mandat-lettre (*nm*) a postal order, with space for writing on it, which the payee can cash in person at the post office

mandat-poste (*nm*) a postal order, money order

mandat simple (*nm*) a permission to sell; a written authorization, given by the seller of a property to an estate agent, authorizing the sale of a property. Such an authorization is compulsory in French law. *See* **authorisation**, **mandat exclusif**

mandataire (*nm/f*) a legal representative, proxy, or attorney

mandement (*nm*) a court order requiring someone connected with the case to carry out a given task, or requiring the presentation before the court of certain documents. A form of subpoena. *See* **commission rogatoire**

marge (*nf*) a margin (on a form). **faire des annotations en marge** to make notes in the margin. *See* **émargement**

mariage (*nm*) a marriage, wedding ceremony. In France the church cannot legally marry couples. That duty is performed by the State, in the person of the mayor (**maire**) at the town hall (**mairie**). Many couples do go through a church ceremony later, but this is a symbolic act only, without legal validity. The minimum legal age for marriage is 18 for a man and 15 for a woman. The State also gives legal recognition to common-law marriages and cohabitation. *See below and* **allocation, communauté, concubinage, livret de famille, loi Méhaignerie**

mariage civil (*nm*) a civil or registry office marriage. All French marriages are civil affairs, conducted in the town hall (**mairie**) by the mayor or assistant mayor. A church marriage (**mariage religieux**), if required, follows the civil ceremony, but is, in legal terms, only a symbolic act of solemnization.

mariage religieux (*nm*) a church wedding, solemnization of a wedding in church. *See above*

mastère (*nf*) a postgraduate qualification, not counted as a degree. *See* **Diplôme d'Etudes Universitaires Générales, magistère, maîtrise**

maternelle (*nf*) *short for* **école maternelle** nursery school or playschool

maternité (*nf*) (1) pregnancy (2) a maternity hospital. **allocation de maternité** maternity allowance. *See* **allocation**

matrice cadastrale (*nf*) a land register, a list of who owns what, available for inspection at the town hall (**mairie**)

Me. a form of written address in a letter to a lawyer, a shortened form of **maître. Cher Me. Martin** Dear Mr Martin

médaille d'honneur du travail (*nf*) a long-service award given to employees, rather in the spirit in which gold watches are presented in Britain

médiation (*nf*) arbitration, dispute settling. **médiation familiale** marriage guidance. **médiation pénale** a formal attempt to arrange compensation between the author and victim of a criminal act, prior to the case coming to court. This mediation is usually carried out under the supervision of the ministry of justice. *See* **arbitrage**

mensonger/ère (*adj*) false, untrue, misleading, deceitful.

déposition mensongère false evidence, perjury. *See* **dol, parjure, publicité mensongère, serment**

métier (*nm*) profession, occupation, trade. *See* **cadre, chambre des métiers, régime complémentaire**

métro (*nm*) underground railway. Paris has the best and largest, but there are smaller versions in Bordeaux, Lille, Lyon, Marseille and Toulouse. *See* **carte, RER**

métropole (*nf*) mainland France, a term used to distinguish mainland France from its overseas colonies and **départements (DOM/TOM)**. *See* **hexagone**

mettre (*vb*) to put, set. *See* **mise**

meublé/e (*adj*) furnished (flat). French rented accommodation is usually unfurnished, though often with the exception of a furnished kitchen (**cuisine équipée**).

mineur émancipé (*nm*) *see* **émancipation**

minitel (*nm*) the computerized telephone directory available since 1984 at a terminal in post offices. Telephone subscribers are provided with **minitel** free of charge. For a fee, users also have access to 12,000 different services, including banking facilities, travel arrangements, theatre bookings, train reservations, weather forecasts, offers of jobs, and accommodation. *See* **télétel**

mise (*nf*) putting, setting. A very common word used in all kinds of phrases. *See below*

> **mise à jour** (*nf*) an updating, in the sense of an additional document or appendix containing recent information. *See* **annexe, avenant**

> **mise à pied** (*nf*) suspension from work (of an employee by the employer, usually following a disciplinary offence). *See* **congé, licenciement, préavis**

> **mise aux voix** (*nf*) putting to the vote

> **mise de fonds** (*nf*) capital outlay, initial costs

> **mise en accusation** (*nf*) a preliminary summons, usually issued by the **Procureur de la République** in a *criminal*

case, informing someone that they are the subject of proceedings. *See* **assignation, citation directe, comparution**

mise en cause (*nf*) a formal investigation. The decision of an examining magistrate (**juge d'instruction**) to proceed with a full investigation of someone suspected of having committed an offence

mise en demeure (*nf*) a formal demand or instruction. **mettre qn en demeure de faire qch** (1) to instruct or order someone to do something (2) to give someone formal notice to do something (such as pay a fine). *See* **avis, congé, préavis**

mise en disponibilité (*nf*) leave of absence (in the Civil Service)

mise en état (*nf*) *see* **juge de la mise en état**

mise en garde (*nf*) a formal warning. *See* **mise en demeure**

mise en valeur (*nf*) (1) development (of a building plot) (2) improvement, revamping, repair (of a property). *See* **restaurer**

mitoyenneté (*nf*) (1) shared responsibility for the upkeep of a common boundary (2) the planning restrictions or obligations which result from a shared boundary, such as the duty not to block out the light from neighbours' windows. *See* **bornage, copropriété**

Modulopass (*nm*) a railcard offering cut-price travel

montant (*nm*) an amount, sum, total (of money)

moratoire (*adj*) moratory. **intérêts moratoires** interest on arrears, back interest

motif (*nm*) grounds, justification. A lawyer will often introduce his conclusions with **Par ces motifs** ... 'On these grounds ...'

motif de l'appel (*nm*) the purpose of the recruitment of or job offer to (an employee of a fixed-term contract of employment). The grounds on which an employer can recruit staff to fixed-term contracts are strictly limited by the **Code du Travail** (*ART.L.122-1-1*). These are: as a replacement for a permanent employee temporarily absent or not yet arrived in post; a temporary increase in the normal business of the enterprise; seasonal activity. *See* **contrat de travail à durée déterminée, requalification, vices de consentement**

moyen (*nm*) a legal argument or ground, in support of a petition. **soulever un moyen** to put forward an argument

mutilé de (la) guerre (*nm*) disabled ex-serviceman. *See* **grand invalide de guerre**

mutualité (*nf*) mutual benefit insurance

mutuelle (*nf*) mutual benefit insurance company, friendly society. A voluntary insurance scheme, normally only open to people who satisfy special conditions such as belonging to a certain occupation, which offers additional cover for things like medical expenses. They also offer schemes for children's holiday camps.

nationalité (*nf*) nationality. An immigrant can apply for French nationality after being resident in France for five years. Someone married to a French national can apply after six months.

négotiation obligatoire (*nf*) the legal obligation on employers to enter into yearly discussions with their employees over pay and conditions

net/nette (*adj*) *see* **brut**

nom (*nm*) a name. The usual French way of referring to a person's name is to ask for **nom et prénom**, (sur)name and first name. When written, the surname is spelled out in capitals, the first name in small letters, with the surname written first, as in Louis Malle's film *LACOMBE Lucien*. *See below and* **coordonnées**, **surnom**

   nom de baptême (*nm*) a Christian name. *More usually* **prénom**. *See* **petit nom**

nom de famille (*nm*) a surname

nom de femme mariée (*nm*) a married name

nom de jeune fille (*nm*) a maiden name

nom de marque (*nm*) a (registered) trademark

non-comparution (*nf*) the failure of someone to turn up, or present him- or herself, before an official body, such as a court. *See* **défaut**

non-concurrence (*nf*) *see* **engagement de non-concurrence**

non-décès (*nm*) *see* **déclaration de non-décès**

non-garantie (*nf*) a **clause de non-garantie** is a non-guarantee clause, or the opposite of a guarantee. It frees someone of all future responsibility for something, usually in the context of a seller denying responsibility for defects that may emerge later in the thing being sold.

non-lieu (*nm*) withdrawal of case. The decision by a court or **juge d'instruction** not to proceed with a prosecution. *See* **débouter**

non-titulaires (*nm.pl*) people employed by the State but without the long-term security, status or benefits of permanent full-time employees (or **fonctionnaires titulaires**). Almost one-third of all state employees fall into this category, whose three main groupings are **auxiliaires, contractuels** and **vacataires**.

notaire (*nm*) roughly equivalent to a solicitor, able to give legal advice, authenticate documents and to oversee the buying and selling of property, but who does not represent clients in court, work which is done only by an **avocat** or **avoué**. *See* **acte authentique, barème, barreau, frais de notaire**

notarié/e (*adj*) (of a document, etc.) prepared or drawn up by a solicitor. *See above and* **acte authentique, papier timbré**

note (*nf*) (1) a bill (in a restaurant, etc.)   (2) a (written) note   (3) a mark (in an exam, etc.)

note de service (*nf*) a memo

note honoraires (*nf*) a bill for fees (from a lawyer, etc.)

notoire (*adj*) well known, of public knowledge. A false friend. *See below*

notoriété (*nf*) the state of being common knowledge. A false friend, it does not necessarily carry the negative overtones of the English 'notorious'. **la notoriété d'un concubinage** the common knowledge that a certain couple live together as man and wife. *See above and* **acte de notoriété**

nul/nulle (*adj*) null and void, invalid. **nul et non avenu** null and void. **rendre nul** to annul, nullify. *See* **caduc, dol**

nullité (*nf*) nullity, invalidity, the state of being null and void. *See* **caducité**

numéro vert (*nm*) a free-phone telephone number. Equivalent to an 0800 number in Britain

obligation alimentaire (*nf*) the legal obligation of adult children, grandchildren and other close relatives to look after elderly people. When an old person applies for financial help from the State, not only their own, but also their relatives' financial situation is closely examined, often in minute detail, down to the amount of food grown in the greenhouse. *See* **recouvrement par succession**

occupation des sols (*nf*) *see* **plan d'occupation des sols**

Office National d'Information sur les Enseignements et les Professions (*nm*) a national careers advice service with offices throughout the country, which also runs the **centres d'information et d'orientation** and the **conseillers d'orientation**

officier de l'état civil (*nm*) a registrar; the role is often filled by the mayor (**maire**) or one of his or her deputies (at occasions such as marriages)

officier de paix (*nm*) a senior officer in the uniformed branch of the police, who are known collectively as **gardiens de la paix**. *See* **gendarme**

officier de police (*nm*) a police officer. Also called **agent de police**

officier public (*nm*) an official empowered to authenticate legal documents. *See* **notoriété**

omnibus (*nm*) a train which halts at every stop

ordonnance (*nf*) (1) a prescription issued by a doctor (2) a legislative ruling made by the government as opposed to Parliament, and which has not gone through the normal law-making process   (3) a (court) order or ruling

ordre des avocats (*nm*) the group of **avocats** listed as members of a particular bar (**barreau**)

ordre des géomètres-experts (*nm*) the registry of surveyors. *See* **géomètre-expert**

orientation (*nf*) careers advice. **orientation scolaire** advice to schoolchildren and their parents about the choice of academic subjects, usually given by the school careers officer (**conseiller d'orientation**)

ouvrier/ouvrière (*nm/f*) a worker, usually in a manual occupation. Though foreign workers are referred to as **travailleurs étrangers**, the usual way to refer to non-manual workers is **le personnel** or **les salariés**. French workers tend to be jealous of their status. A **fonctionnaire** would be mortified to be called an **employé**, and a **cadre** would be insulted to be referred to by another title. This concern is shown in the case of the **ouvrier spécialisé** who, contrary to implication, is one of the lowest grades of employee, usually in unskilled manual work.

paie (*nf*) pay, wages. Those who are paid monthly prefer **salaire** (salary).

palais (*nm*) a large hall, exhibition hall

palais de justice (*nm*) the law courts

papier timbré (*nm*) a legal document on which stamp duty has been paid and which is used for legally binding agreements

paraphe (*nm*) (personal) initials (standing as signature). *See* **émargement**

parapher (*vb*) to initial (a cheque, etc.). *See* **émarger, endosser**

parjure (*nm*) perjury, false evidence, lying in court. *See* **dénonciation calomnieuse, faux témoignage**

parquet (*nm*) see **juge, magistrat**

particulier (*nm*) a private individual, private person. *Particulier à Particulier* is a well-known magazine for private individuals offering properties for sale or rent.

particulier/ière (*adj*) (1) private, belonging to a private person (of a car, etc.)   (2) exceptional, special (of circumstances, etc.). *See* **exceptionnellement**

partie adversaire (*nf*) see **adversaire**

parvenir (*vb*) to reach. **faire parvenir** to send (a package, etc.). **je vous serais reconnaissant de bien vouloir me faire parvenir** ... (in a letter) I would be most grateful if you would send me ... *See* **communication, lettre recommandée**

passer en justice (*vb*) to stand trial. *See* **aller en justice, saisir la justice**

patrimoine (*nm*) an inheritance, patrimony, goods left in a will

patron (*nm*) an owner, boss. *See* **chef, gérant, propriétaire**

patronal (*adj*) relating to employers. *See* **prêt patronal, syndicat patronal**

patronat (*nm*) an umbrella term for employers; the bosses. Opposite of **salariat**

paysan/paysanne (*nm/f*) a peasant. **Paysan** in French culture implies something far more noble than its English translation suggests. It normally refers to a small, independent farmer. To many, the country dweller remains the soul of France, whose decline through the great postwar migrations to the cities is viewed with regret. The **paysans** are proud of their status and have their own organizations. There is middle-class chic in being able to point to **paysan** origins.

péage (*nm*) a toll, or toll-booth (on a motorway, etc.). *See* **autoroute**

peine (*nf*) punishment. *See* **amende**

pension (*nf*) (1) a pension (2) a boarding-house (3) a boarding-school (4) board and lodgings. **demi-pension** half-board

> **pension alimentaire** (*nf*) (1) maintenance, alimony (following divorce) (2) a (student's) living allowance. *See* **aliments, obligation alimentaire**

> **pension d'invalidité** (*nf*) a disablement pension

> **pension de retraite** (*nf*) a retirement pension. *See* **assurance, régimes d'assurance vieillesse**

> **pension de reversion** (*nf*) the arrangement by which part of a person's pension continues to be paid to his or her partner after death. *See* **droits dérivés**

percepteur (*nm*) a tax collector

perception (*nf*) (1) collection (of taxes, fines, etc.) (2) a tax collector's office

péréquation (*nf*) (1) adjustment, realignment, upgrading (of salaries or pensions that need to be index-linked) (2) balancing out (of costs, taxes)

période blanche (*nf*) a regular peak period (for trains, etc.). *See* **carte** *and below*

période bleue (*nf*) off-peak period, when most concessions are available

période rouge (*nf*) high peak period (in travel)

permanent (*nm*) a full-time union official

permis (*nm*) a licence, permit. *See below*

> **permis de chasse** (*nm*) a hunting permit (hunting without one is illegal)

permis de conduire (*nm*) a driving licence. The driving test is in two parts, the first written, the second a practical test of driving skill. A full driving licence cannot be gained before the age of 18, but the written part of the test can be taken at the age of 16, which allows an under-18 to take the wheel when accompanied by a qualified driver. However, the *type* of driver who is allowed to accompany learners is strictly controlled. *See* **conduite accompagnée**. *See also* **alcool au volant**, **auto-école**, **immatriculation**

permis de construire (*nm*) planning or building permission, obtained from the town hall (**mairie**). *See* **certificat d'urbanisme**, **mitoyenneté**, **plan d'occupation des sols**, **servitudes**, **terrain**, **viabilisé**

permis de pêche (*nm*) a fishing permit, which must be obtained through the local branch of the fishing association (**Association Agréée de Pêche et de Pisciculture**). There is also a fishing tax to pay, the **taxe piscicole**.

permis de séjour (*nm*) *same as* **carte de séjour**

permis de travail (*nm*) a work permit, needed only by non-EU nationals. This is applied for by the prospective employer. If granted, the prospective employee is given a **visa de long séjour** lasting for up to three months. Once this is obtained, the employee can apply for a **carte de séjour.**

perquisition (*nf*) a formal search of a person or premises (by police, customs, etc.). *See* **fouille**, **mandat**

perquisitionner (*vb.int*) to carry out a formal search

personne civile (*nf*) *same as* **personne juridique**

personne juridique (*nf*) a person, in the context of the law. That is to say, someone who is subject to the law, enjoying rights, duties and obligations. All human beings fall into this category. A legal person. *See below*

personne morale (*nf*) (in law) a corporate personality, or corporation. A group of people or a company, such as a **société anonyme**, which, for the purposes of law, is to be treated as the equivalent of a person, having rights, duties and obligations. A **personne morale** is one type of **personne juridique**. *See above and below*

personne physique (*nf*) (in law) an individual. A natural person

personnel (le) (*nm*) staff. *See* **effectif, ouvrier**

petit nom (*nm*) a Christian name, first name, forename. *See* **nom**

pharmacie (*nf*) a chemist's shop. **pharmacie de garde** a duty chemist, all-night chemist

pièce (*nf*) (1) a room. **trois pièces** a three-room flat. (2) a coin (3) a document. **pièce officielle** an official document, such as a birth certificate, that can be used to prove a statement or entitlement. *See* **ampliation, communication (de pièces), état civil, extrait**

piston (*nm*) a slang term for the old boy network, friends in the right places, string-pulling. **obtenir un poste par le piston** to get a job through contacts. *See* **système D**

placement (*nf*) (1) an investment (2) a placement, posting, positioning (of staff in a business). **agence de placement** an employment agency

plaider (*vb*) (1) to plead (a case in court), to present a case verbally (2) to go to court (of a barrister). *See* **comparution, convocation, ester en justice, plaidoirie, poursuivre qn en justice**

plaideur/plaideuse (*nm/f*) a litigant, someone taking a case to court. *See* **demandeur**

plaidoirie (*nf*) a barrister's speech to the court

plainte (*nf*) a formal complaint. **déposer plainte contre qn** to make a complaint against someone

plan (*nm*) (1) a map (2) a plan (3) a blueprint (4) a programme (of development)

plan d'occupation des sols (*nm*) local planning regulations. Each **mairie** has available a set of guidelines covering the different uses to which land within the **commune** can be put.

See **coefficient d'occupation du sol, déclaration préalable de construction, mitoyenneté, permis de construire, servitudes, urbanisme**

pli non-urgent (*nm*) an item sent by post, declared as non-urgent mail and so charged at a lower rate. *See* **franchise**

plus-value (*nf*) (1) appreciation, increase in value (of property, investments, etc.) (2) a (budget) surplus, profit. **impôt sur les plus-values** capital gains tax

police (*nf*) (1) an insurance policy (2) regulations (3) police. **agent de police** a policeman or -woman. **poste de police** a police station. *See below and* **commissaire, commissariat, gardien de la paix, gendarme, officier de paix**

   police de l'air et des frontières (*nf*) customs and immigration police. A branch of the **police nationale** who also supervise immigration checks and air and rail crashes

   police judiciaire (*nf*) a specialist unit under the control of the **Procureur de la République**, made up of officers from the **gendarmerie** and **police nationale**, who investigate organized crime

   police municipale (*nf*) the local (town) police, normally restricted to minor police tasks. Not to be confused with the **police urbaine**, city or town police, who are detachments of the **police nationale** assigned to larger towns

   police nationale (*nf*) the national police force, whose two main branches are the **police urbaine** and the **CRS (Compagnies Républicaines de Sécurité)**. Distinct from the **Gendarmerie Nationale**, who, although carrying out police work, are part of the defence ministry

   police urbaine (*nf*) city or town police. *See above*

polytechnique (*adj*) *see* **Ecole Polytechnique**

pompes funèbres (*nf.pl*) (1) the office of an undertaker or funeral director (2) the act of making arrangements for the dead. Funerals can be undertaken either by private companies of undertakers or by the local authority (**commune**). *See* **décès, recouvrement par succession**

poste (*nf*) the Post Office (organization). Its official title is now **PT (Postes et Téléphones)**, but it is still better known as the **PTT (Postes, Télégraphes et Téléphones)**, the initials which continue to appear on many buildings. An individual post office is **un bureau de poste**, though it is usual, if asking directions, to ask for the **PTT**. *See* **courrier, lettre recommandée, mandat, timbre-taxe**

poste restante (*nf*) poste restante. Mail is addressed to a post office and held for a minimum of two weeks, to allow the addressee to pick it up. This is particularly useful during the holidays or when looking for work.

postéclair (*nf*) the fax service run by **France-Télécom**

pouponnière (*nf*) a day nursery, normally for children under 3. *See* **centre aéré, colonie de vacances, crèche, école maternelle, halte-garderie**

poursuivre qn en justice (*vb*) to prosecute, take legal action against, take someone to court. *See* **actionner, assigner, ester en justice**

pourvoi en cassation (*nm*) an appeal (in a court case), referral to the court of appeal (**cour de cassation**)

pouvoir (*nm*) a mandate, authority, proxy. **donner pouvoir à qn de faire qch** to give someone authority to do something. *See below and* **autorisation**

　　pouvoir par-devant notaire (*nm*) a power of attorney

　　pouvoir spécial de représentation (*nm*) a written authorization for one person to act on another's behalf (in an industrial tribunal, etc.). *See above and below*

préalable (*adj*) **préalable à** (1) prior to, before (2) as a precondition of (signing a contract, etc.). *See* **clause suspensive, contrat de travail, réserve**

préalablement à (*adv*) beforehand, as a (necessary) prelude to, firstly. **préalablement à faire qch** prior to doing something

préavis (*nm*) an (advance) notice. **un préavis de deux jours** two days' notice. **préavis de grève** notice of going on strike. *See* **congé**

précaire (*adj*) precarious, lacking security, not permanent, without security of tenure. Applied to short-term contracts of employment. *See* **précarité**

précarité (*nf*) (of employment) the state of being precarious (**précaire**) or of lacking security. **La prime de précarité** is a special bonus payment, amounting to around 5 per cent of earnings. All employees are legally entitled to this payment when they reach the end of a fixed-term or temporary contract. *See* **auxiliaire**, **contrat de travail à durée déterminée**, **précaire**, **travail temporaire**

préfecture (*nf*) the (equivalent of) county hall, administrative headquarters of a **département**. *See* **cité administrative**. **préfecture de police** police headquarters. *See* **commissariat de police**

préfet (*nm*) the senior government officer in a **département**, who is not elected by the population but appointed by the President. Responsible for carrying out government policy in the area, his or her deputies are known as **sous-préfets**, deputy or under-prefects. There is also a **préfet de région** who performs a similar role at regional level. *See* **région**

préjudice (*nm*) injury, damage, loss, harm. A false friend. **au préjudice de Monsieur Martin** to the detriment of Mr Martin. **porter préjudice à qn** to harm, cause loss or injury to someone, to harm the interests of someone. **subir un préjudice** to suffer loss or damage

prélèvement (*nm*) a deduction, levy, withdrawal. **prélèvement bancaire** a banker's or standing order. **prélèvement libératoire** payment of tax by standing order which deducts it directly from the dividend on investments, an arrangement which can produce tax benefits. *See* **cotisation**

premier cycle (*nm*) years one and two in higher education, the completion of which can become a qualification in its own right, the **Diplôme d'Etudes Universitaires Générales (DEUG)**

premier tour (*nm*) the first round of voting in French elections. If a candidate fails to win a majority on the first ballot, a second ballot (**second tour**) is held a week later, minus those who polled badly, allowing their supporters to transfer their votes.

prénom (*nm*) a first name, Christian name. *See* **nom**

préparation militaire (*nf*) a voluntary period of training in advance of national service (**service militaire**)

prescription (*nf*) a time limit within which an action must be carried out. **la prescription de la peine** the statute of limitations – the time limit within which a punishment must be pronounced. These are: for **crimes** twenty years, for **délits** five years, for **contraventions** two years. (Note, a chemist's prescription is an **ordonnance**.) *See* **délai**

président (*nm*) (1) (in a court) the president   (2) (in business) the chairman or president of a company   (3) (in politics) the President

prestation (*nf*) (1) service (in a hotel, etc.)   (2) a performance (in a theatre, etc.)   (3) swearing (an oath). **prestation de serment** taking an oath   (4) a benefit, allowance. *See below and* **allocation**

    prestation d'invalidité (*nf*) invalidity benefit

    prestation en nature (*nf*) *same as* **avantages en nature**

    prestations familiales (*nf.pl*) (the whole range of) family benefits paid by the State, such as child benefit and maternity benefit

prêt conventionné (*nm*) a mortgage or loan for buying or building *new* property, as opposed to **prêt pour l'accession à la propriété**, a mortgage or loan for the buying or renovation of an existing property. *See* **hypothèque**

prêt d'épargne-logement (*nm*) a loan or mortgage for property, usually only up to a limited amount and linked to having been a saver for a certain period in a **compte épargne-logement**

prêt patronal (*nm*) a part loan for property-buying given by an employer. *See* **aide personnalisée au logement**, **emprunt**, **hypothèque**

prêt pour l'accession à la propriété (*nm*) *see* **prêt conventionné**

prétensions (*nf.pl*) a false friend. (1) an expected or hoped-for salary when applying for a job. **quelles sont vos prétensions?** what kind of salary are you looking for? (2) claims or demands (in a court case)

preuves (*nf.pl*) proof, evidence. **preuves écrites** written proof. **documents-preuves** documentary evidence. *See* **écrit**

prévention (*nf*) (1) custody, detention, remand (2) prejudice, bias. *See* **détention**, **garde à vue**, **interpellation**, **liberté surveillée**, **prison préventative**

prévention routière (*nf*) road safety

prévenu/e (*nm/f*) the term for the accused or defendant when appearing before a judge. *See* **accusé**

prévoyance (*nf*) foresight, forethought. **caisse de prévoyance** contingency fund, emergency reserve. **société de prévoyance** provident society. *See* **Caisse d'Epargne et de Prévoyance**, **fonds de roulement**

prime (*nf*) an allowance, subsidy, bonus. *See* **allocation**, **indemnité**, **subvention**

    prime à l'amélioration de l'habitat (*nf*) a home-improvement grant, paid by the local authority via the town hall (**mairie**)

    prime d'assiduité (*nf*) a loyalty, good conduct or punctuality bonus paid by an employer to an employee, for example, at the end of a temporary contract

    prime de déménagement (*nf*) a grant awarded to a family with three or more children (**famille nombreuse**) moving home within two years of the birth of a child. *See* **aide personnalisée au logement**, **allocation logement**

    prime de précarité (*nf*) *see* **précarité**

    prime de transport (*nf*) a travel allowance

prison préventative (*nf*) (police) custody. **faire de prison préventative** to be in custody. *See* **prévention**

procédure (*nf*) (1) proceedings (in a court, etc.) (2) procedure, rules of procedure (3) the totality of formalities or steps which must be completed before the hearing of a case before a judge. *See below and* **cour**, **juge**, **juridiction**, **tribunal**

procédure à jour (*nf*) an emergency hearing (in a court, etc.). In exceptional circumstances, a plaintiff may make a direct appeal to a judge to fix an early date for a hearing, and so by-pass normal procedure.

procédure civile (*nf*) civil proceedings, an action brought in a civil court, as opposed to a criminal court

procédure pénale (*nf*) criminal proceedings, a prosecution in a criminal court. *See above*

procès (*nm*) a trial, proceedings, court case

procès d'intention (*nm*) a legal action where someone is sued for their *intention* to do something, as distinct from something they have already done. *See* **tierce opposition**

procès-verbal (*nm*) a statement, report, minutes. **dresser un procès-verbal contre qn** (of police) to book or report someone

procuration (*nf*) a proxy, power of attorney, authorization to act on someone else's behalf. *See* **autorisation**, **désigné**, **mandat**, **pouvoir**

procureur (*nm*) the prosecuting lawyer acting for the State; public prosecutor. **procureur-adjoint** an assistant prosecutor. *See* **cour**, **juge**, **tribunal**

Procureur de la République (*nm*) a public or state prosecutor. *See* **juge d'instruction**, **police judiciaire**

professeur (*nm*) (general term for) a teacher. *See also* **auxiliaire**, **instituteur**, **maître de conférences**

professeur agrégé (*nm*) a teacher who holds an **agrégation**

professeur certifié (*nm*) a teacher who holds a **CAPES**

programme à loyer réduit (*nm*) a form of subsidized housing. *See* **logement social**

promesse bilatérale (*nf*) *same as* **promesse de vente synallagmatique**

promesse de vente (nf) a promise to buy (by the buyer) and sell (by the seller). There are various forms of this pre-contract agreement. *See below and* **acte de vente, compromis de vente, contrat de réservation, indemnité d'immobilisation, promesse bilatérale**

    promesse de vente avec dédit (nf) *same as* **compromis de vente** and **promesse de vente synallagmatique**

    promesse de vente fermée (nf) *same as* **promesse unilatérale de vente**

    promesse de vente synallagmatique (nf) in house-buying, an agreement to buy and sell. The buyer places a deposit (**indemnité d'immobilisation**). Should the sale fall through for reasons other than those permitted in the contract, the party responsible must pay a forfeit. If the buyer is responsible, the deposit is forfeited; if the seller is responsible, *double* the deposit must be returned to the buyer. *Also known as* **compromis de vente, promesse de vente avec dédit** *or* **promesse bilatérale**

    promesse unilatérale de vente (nf) a contract for the sale of a property, in which the seller agrees to sell and the buyer agrees to buy. The buyer puts down a deposit of up to 10 per cent, with a period during which either side may withdraw from the agreement. If it is the buyer who backs out, the deposit is lost. After this period, the contract becomes binding. *Also known as a* **promesse de vente fermée**

propriétaire (nm/f) (1) an owner, proprietor (of a house or business) (2) a landlord (as opposed to tenant). **propriétaire-foncier** a landowner. *See* **locataire**

proviseur (nm) the headmaster or headmistress of a **lycée**

provision (nf) (1) stock, supply (of goods, water, etc.) (2) a retainer, retaining fee (paid to a solicitor, etc.) (3) a deposit (in house-buying, etc.). *See* **arrhes**. (4) funds available (in a bank account). *See* **chèque sans provision**

prud'hommal (adj) relating to or concerning the **Conseil de Prud'hommes**

Prud'hommes (nm.pl) *see* **Conseil de Prud'hommes**

PT, PTT the Post Office. *See* **poste**

publicité mensongère (*nf*) fraudulent, or misleading, advertising. In particular, according to *Article.L.311-4* of the **Code du Travail**, 'It is illegal to publish in a newspaper, magazine or periodical offers of employment, ... containing claims which are false or liable to mislead, particularly in regard to one or more of the following: the existence, origin or description of the post, or ... its rate of pay, benefits or place of work.' *See* **commission des clauses abusives**, **Conseil de Prud'hommes**, **DDCCRF**, **dol**, **nul**

pupille de l'Etat (*nm/f*) a child in care. *See* **Direction Départementale de l'Action Sanitaire et Sociale**

quart (*nm*) *see* **roulement, travail**

quasi-délit (*nm*) *see* **infraction**

quittance (*nf*) a receipt, particularly in the sense of one for the discharge or final payment of money owed. **quittance de loyer** (*nf*) a rent receipt, proof of payment of rent. Sometimes asked for among other pieces of ID. *See* **caution**, **dépôt de garantie**, **récépissé**, **timbre-quittance**

quotient familial (*nm*) a kind of family tax rating used for a variety of purposes, including tax assessment and the amount to be paid by parents towards school dinners for their children

radiation (*nf*) (1) the act of removing someone's name from an official list (of members, etc.) (2) the act of cancelling someone's entitlement to something (such as social security benefits) (3) striking off, or disbarring (of a lawyer, etc.). **avis de radiation** formal notice of being struck off a list

radier (*vb*) (1) to strike off the register   (2) to disbar. *See* **blâme**

rallonge (*nf*) (1) an extension (for an electric plug, etc.)   (2) a supplement. **une rallonge de deux jours** a two-day extension. *See* **annexe, avenant, délai**

ramassage (*nm*) picking up, collection. **ramassage scolaire** a school bus (service). **point de ramassage** a school bus stop. French school buses are outstanding. They are plentiful and accompanied by local policemen (**gardes champêtres**), who wait at every stop to help the children across the road.

ramonage (*nm*) chimney-sweeping, (boiler) flue-cleaning. Because of explosions caused by blocked boiler chimneys and flues, insurance companies insist on all chimneys being professionally cleaned before insuring house contents. This can only be done by an officially approved chimney-sweep (**agréé par l'Etat**), who issues a **certificat de ramonage**.

ramoneur (*nm*) a chimney-sweep

rapport (*nm*) a report. *See* **juge rapporteur**

rapporter (*vb*) (1) to bring back   (2) to yield a return (of shares, investments). **les actions lui rapportaient beaucoup d'argent** his shares brought him in a lot of money   (3) to report, make a report   (4) to add on (an extension to a house, etc.). *See* **constat**

ratification (*nf*) ratification, formal confirmation. **ratification de vente** confirmation of sale

récépissé (*nm*) (1) a warrant   (2) a receipt, in the sense of one given to confirm the deposit of valuables, such as by a hotel manager to a guest who leaves valuables to be locked in the safe

réclame (*nf*) advertising, an advertisement. **en réclame** on special offer, on special promotion (of goods in a shop, etc.)

reconnaissant/e (*adj*) grateful. *See* **parvenir**

reconventionnel/le (*adj*) counter. *See* **demande reconventionnelle**

recours (*nm*) an appeal (in court), recourse. *See below*

    recours contentieux (*nm*) a proposal for an out-of-court settlement. *See* **amiable, arbitrage, conciliation**

recours en cassation (*nm*) an appeal to the Supreme Court

recours gracieux (*nm*) (1) a request for a legal ruling or judgement (in court). This is distinct from a **recours en grâce**, which is specifically a plea for clemency made by a convicted person to the President of France (2) an appeal for more lenient terms, for example, asking the tax office to agree to the payment of a tax demand by instalments

recouvrement (*nm*) (1) collection, payment (of tax, etc.) (2) recovery (of debt). *See* **cotisation, impôt, perception**

recouvrement de créance (*nm*) debt collection

recouvrement par succession (*nm*) the right of the local authorities to claim back from the estates of deceased people the cost of financial and other help given to them while they were alive. *See* **aide ménagère, obligation alimentaire, testament**

rectorat (*nm*) (1) the (local) education offices (2) a rectorship (in a university, etc.), referring either to the position itself or its term of office

reçu (*nm*) a receipt. *See* **récépissé, solde de tout compte**

récuser (*vb*) to ask that a judge or official stand down because of lack of impartiality. *See* **suspicion légitime**

redevance (*nf*) (1) a licence (for TV, etc.) (2) a rental charge (3) fees due (4) tax. *See* **abonnement, impôt**

redoublement (*nm*) repeating a year, having to take a course again (in a school, etc.)

regard (*nm*) (1) a viewing hole or window (in a boiler, etc.) (2) a small manhole giving access to the water main or stop-cock. *See* **équipement, service des eaux**

régie (*nf*) (1) a state-controlled industry (2) state control (3) local authority control

régime (*nm*) (1) a system (2) regulations. **régime douanier** customs regulations (3) a scheme (of Social Security). *See below and* **communauté**

régime matrimonial (*nm*) a marriage agreement, marriage contract, marriage settlement. *Not* the same as a marriage certificate (**extrait d'acte de mariage**) or marriage licence (**dispense de bans**). There are many different forms of marriage agreement. *See* **communauté**

régimes d'assurance vieillesse (*nm.pl*) pension schemes. The French **Sécurité Sociale** uses a three-tier system of pension schemes (**assurance vieillesse**):

(1) **régime général** (*nm*) the basic pension scheme, to which all workers are entitled

(2) **régime spécial** (*nm*) a higher-rate pension scheme, linked to a specific occupation. The pension offers considerably higher payments and can be claimed earlier than normal retirement age. However, it is linked to one specific occupation, and so cannot be claimed prematurely if the worker moves to another occupation, though payments will still begin at normal retirement age.

(3) **régime complémentaire** (*nm*) a top-up scheme, complementary scheme. Better-paid professions also operate top-up schemes guaranteeing higher benefits. These are similar to British private or occupational pension schemes, the difference being that they are compulsory for all employees, not voluntary, and that they are tied closely to the State.

région (*nf*) a region, one of twenty administrative segments into which France is divided. Each **région** contains a number of **départements** and is headed by its own **préfet**, who is at the same time **préfet** of one of the **départements**.

région parisienne *see* **Ile de France**

registre de comptabilité (*nm*) a ledger, accountant's ledger. *See* **comptable**

registre de l'état civil (*nm*) a register of births, marriages and deaths

registre du commerce (*nm*) a trade register, register of companies, list of businesses

registre du rôle (*nm*) a list of cases to be heard by the court, a copy of which is hung in the waiting-room; the day's court agenda

registre mortuaire (*nm*) a register of deaths

règlement (*nm*) (1) rules, regulations, rules and regulations. **règlement de copropriété** the rules and regulations governing joint ownership. *See* **déontologie** (2) payment, settlement (of a debt, etc.). **règlement par chèque** payment by cheque (3) **règlement judiciaire** compulsory liquidation, enforced winding up (of a business). *See* **astreinte, faillite**

réglementation (*nf*) regulations, rules and regulations, regulation, control

  réglementation de travail (*nf*) work regulations. *See* **carte de résident, carte de séjour, convention collective, Inspection du Travail, permis de travail**

régler (*vb*) to settle or pay up (a bill, an account). *See* **compte, faillite**

régulariser (*vb*) to straighten out, sort out, or put in order, particularly in an administrative sense. **régulariser votre situation** to become officially registered, to fill in the appropriate paperwork. **régulariser vos papiers** to get your papers in order. *See* **irrégulier, travail clandestin**

régulier/ière (*adj*) in order, above-board. **être en situation régulière** to have everything legally in order, to be in line with the law. *Opposite of a* **situation irrégulière**. *See* **irrégulier**

relevé (*nm*) a statement or summary (of account, etc.). *See below*

  relevé bancaire (*nm*) a bank statement

  relevé de compte (*nm*) a bank statement, balance

  relevé de condamnation (*nm*) a police record. *See* **casier, déclaration de non-condamnation**

  relevé d'identité bancaire (*nm*) a bank ID. This has no exact English equivalent, but refers to a proof of identity as supplied by a bank. This is normally a slip in the back of a cheque-book carrying one's bank details. It is often asked for as a proof of ID.

renouvellement (*nm*) renewal (of a contract). *See* **avenant, contrat de travail, contrat verbal**

renseignements (*nm.pl*) information. **fournir des renseignements sur** to give details or particulars of. *See* **attestation, coordonnées, répondant**

rente viagère (*nf*) the practice of mortgaging or selling a property in return for a life income or a lump sum, while still remaining a lifelong tenant. The buyer of the property becomes the official owner, but pays a low price, only a proportion (25–33 per cent) of the value, and allows the seller to continue to live in it and to receive regular additional payments for the rest of his or her life. The property reverts to the buyer on the seller's death. It has been called a form of gambling, in which the buyer risks a quick bargain against the life expectancy of the seller. *See* **cession-bail, démembrement de propriété, fonds de commerce, franchise, secours viager, usufruit, viager**

rentrée (*nf*) return (1) the start of the new school year in September, which is given much higher prominence in France than in Britain, perhaps because it coincides with (2) the end of the summer holidays, involving massive traffic jams as everyone returns to the big cities simultaneously. Some attempts are now made to stagger school holidays in different parts of the country. *See* **allocation de rentrée scolaire, départ**

renvoi (*nm*) (1) dismissal, expulsion, notice to leave. *See* **congédier, licenciement** (2) a referral, postponement, putting back (of a meeting, etc.) (3) sending back, returning (in all senses). *See* **avis de réception**

renvoyer (*vb*) (1) to dismiss, expel, give someone notice to leave (2) to postpone, put back (3) to refer (a court case to a different court) (4) to send back, return. *See* **renvoi**

répondant/e (*nm/f*) someone who vouches for, or gives a reference for, another person (in regard to a job application, etc.). *See* **attestation, garant**

reporter (*vb*) to postpone, defer, put back

repos obligatoire (*nm*) a compulsory day off. No employer may compel an employee to work more than six days without a break.

requalification (*nf*) requalification; redefinition of the status of (a contractee). According to French employment law, an employee recruited on a fixed-term contract, whose format is found to be irregular, can ask an industrial tribunal to re-class it as a *permanent* contract, with all the safeguards and benefits that entails. *See* **contrat de travail à durée déterminée, dol, motif de l'appel**

requête (*nf*) a petition, formal request, proceedings. *Same as* **demande en justice. requête conjointe** joint proceedings, joint petition, made by two or more people (e.g. by husband and wife seeking a divorce). *See* **conjoint. requête en cassation** an appeal (against a judgement)

RER (*nm*) the **Réseau Express Régional**, the high-speed underground system linking the centre of Paris to the suburbs. *See* **métro**

réseau (*nm*) a network. *See below*

   réseau de banlieue (*nm*) a suburban transport system

   Réseau Express Régional (*nm*) see **RER**

   réseau ferroviaire (*nm*) a rail network

   réseau routier (*nm*) the national road network

   réseau urbain (*nm*) a town or city transport system

réservation (*nf*) a booking, reservation. *See* **caution, contrat de réservation, promesse de vente**

réserve (*nf*) **sous réserve que** on condition that. **sous toutes réserves** subject to reservation, without guarantee of accuracy. *See* **clause suspensive, préalable**

résidence (*nf*) a place of residence. For tax purposes this can mean a temporary abode as opposed to a permanent home. *See* **domicile, foyer**

responsable (*nm/f*) (1) the person in charge (of an office, etc.)   (2) the guilty party, the person responsible for having done something undesirable. *See* **accusé**

ressort (*nm*) (1) jurisdiction, competence, power (of a court)   (2) responsibility. **être de mon ressort** to be my responsibility   (3) **jugement en premier ressort** a judgement or verdict against which it is possible to lodge an appeal. *See* **appel, juridiction, tribunal**

ressources (*nf.pl*) means, resources, available money. **ressources personnelles** personal means, personal finances. *See* **déclaration de ressources**

restaurer (*vb*) **à restaurer** (*adj*) (of a house for sale) in need of restoration. French houses **à restaurer** can sometimes be little more than a ruin. *See* **permis de construire, plan d'occupation des sols, urbanisme**

réticence (*nf*) wilful omission, the deliberate withholding of information. *See* **dol**

retraite (*nf*) retirement. This is normally at the age of 60 for both men and women, though in some public services it is 55.

rétrogradation (*nf*) demotion (of an employee). It is against the law for an employer to force an employee to take a post or carry out work which is inferior in *either* salary *or* status to the one for which he or she was recruited. To do so is classed as *dismissal*, and allows the employee to claim damages, or have the decision reversed by the industrial tribunal (**Conseil de Prud'hommes**). *See* **licenciement**

revenu minimum d'insertion (RMI) (*nm*) income support given to the low-paid to help with lodging and retraining

RMI *see* **revenu minimum d'insertion**

roulement (*nm*) rotation. **travail par roulement** work on a rota system, work in rotation. *See* **travail à quart**

route départementale (*nf*) the equivalent of a B road in Britain, prefixed on maps by the letter D

route nationale (*nf*) the equivalent of an A road, prefixed on maps by the letter N. A motorway is an **autoroute** and is prefixed by the letter A.

SA a limited company. *See* **société anonyme, société anonyme à responsabilité limitée**

saisie (*nf*) seizure (of goods or belongings by a bailiff or **huissier**), confiscation, distress, distraint, attachment. *See below and* **emprise**

    saisie-arrêt (*nf*) distraint, attachment. Seizure of goods for the payment of a debt. *See* **astreinte**

    saisie-conservatoire (*nf*) temporary seizure of goods to prevent their being sold off or otherwise disposed of

    saisie-exécutions (*nf*) distraint, seizure of goods to be sold by court order. *See* **astreinte**

    saisie-immobilière (*nf*) seizure of real estate

saisine (*nf*) the referral of a case to court

saisir la justice (*vb*) to take court action, take a case to court

salaire (*nm*) *see* **paie**

salaire de référence (*nm*) the proportion of a salary that must be paid into a pension scheme in order to obtain a certain level of pension

salaire minimum de croissance (SMIC) (*nm*) the minimum legal hourly wage

salariat (*nm*) a general term for all employees; salaried staff. *See* **patronat**

salarié/e (*nm/f*) a paid employee. *See* **ouvrier**

salle des ventes (*nf*) auction rooms. *See* **commissaire-priseur, dépôt de vente, surenchère, vente aux enchères**

sanction administrative (*nf*) punishments which State officials can mete out to ordinary people without the need of a trial. These are mostly punishments for financial irregularities, but also include taking away driving licences.

SARL *see* **société anonyme à responsabilité limitée**

scolaire (*adj*) relating to school. **âge scolaire** (a child of) school age. **année scolaire** the school year. *See* **assurance scolaire**, **inscription scolaire** *and below*

scolarisation (*nf*) schooling, in the sense of the physical act of sending a child to school rather than educating them. *See below*

scolariser (*vb*) (1) to send someone to school, to provide someone with schooling   (2) to provide a town or an area with schools

scolarité (*nf*) schooling, in the sense of attendance in the school building, rather than the education received there, which is **enseignement**. **les années de scolarité** school years, the years spent at school. *See above and* **certificat de scolarité**, **école**

Scouts de France (*nm.pl*) a Scouts organization, linked to the Catholic Church. *See* **éclaireurs**, **Guides de France**

scrutin (*nm*) ballot, voting. In France, different types of voting are used for different elections. **scrutin secret** a secret ballot. *See below and* **urne**

> **scrutin à mode mixte** (*nm*) a two-round system of voting employing both the **scrutin majoritaire** and the **scrutin proportionnel**

> **scrutin de liste** (*nm*) the list system of voting. *See below*

> **scrutin majoritaire** (*nm*) election by majority vote, usually in cases of a *group* of people to be elected rather than an individual. In this system, one group, party or list of candidates receives all the seats if it wins 50 per cent or more of the vote. If an outright 50 per cent is not achieved, there is a second round of voting where a straight majority wins. *See* **scrutin uninominal**

> **scrutin proportionnel** (*nm*) proportional representation, proportional system of voting, with seats allocated to each party according to the number of votes received, beginning at the top of its list of candidates

scrutin uninominal (nm) voting for individual candidates. A candidate who receives 50 per cent or more of the vote is elected. Otherwise a second round is held in which the candidate with the highest number of votes is the winner. This system is used in, among other elections, the choosing of the President.

séance (nf) a meeting, sitting, session (of a committee, tribunal, etc.). **être en séance** to be in session

second tour (nm) see **premier tour**

secours viager (nm) a widow's or widower's benefit paid to a surviving spouse for life. See **droits dérivés**, **rente viagère**

secrétaire-greffier (nm/f) (the person who is) clerk of the court. *Often just* **greffier**

secrétariat-greffe (nm) the post of, or the room of, the clerk of the court. *Often just* **greffe**

section (nf) a union branch, in a town or area

Section d'Education Spécialisée (SES) (nf) an education department dealing with children with special needs. See **tronc commun**

Sécurité Sociale (nf) Social Security. See **aide sociale**, **allocation**, **assurance**, **retraite**

séjour (nm) a stay, time spent in a place. See **carte de séjour**

semaine légale (nf) the maximum working week. In theory this is thirty-nine hours. In practice it is often very different. See **amplitude journalière**, **durée hebdomadaire maximum du travail**

Sénat (nm) the upper house of the French parliament, whose members (**sénateurs**) represent, and are elected by, the **départements**

sénateur (nm) a member of the **Sénat**

séparation de corps (nf) legal separation of a married couple, preceding, or as an alternative to, divorce. It is pronounced in a court judgement and absolves the couple from the obligation to live together or to be treated as man and wife. *See* **communauté, divorce**

séparation des biens (*nf*) a type of marriage contract in which a couple retain separate ownership of all their belongings. *See* **régime matrimonial**

septennat (*nm*) the seven-year period of office served by the French President (**Président de la République**)

serment (*nm*) an oath. **faux serment** false testimony, perjury. *See* **faux témoignage, parjure**

service des eaux (*nm*) the local water company, also known as the **Compagnie des Eaux**. Water is supplied by a specialist company rather than by the local authorities.

service militaire (*nm*) *Same as* **service national**

service national (*nm*) national service, abolished in 1996. In principle all males between the ages of 18 and 35 were eligible for service, but the normal call-up age was 19. Only about two-thirds of those eligible actually served. Call-up could be delayed or cancelled. Men of dual nationality were among those exempted. *See* **appelé, Gendarmerie Nationale, préparation militaire, trois jours, volontaires du service national**

servitudes (*nf.pl*) building regulations, in the sense of the restrictions on what the owner is allowed to do to a property or plot of land. *See* **plan d'occupation des sols**

SES *see* **Section d'Education Spécialisée**

SGEN *see* **Syndicat Général de l'Education Nationale**

SICOMI *see* **Société Immobilière pour le Commerce et l'Industrie**

signataire (*nm/f*) a signatory, someone who signs a document. *See* **cosignataire, émarger, lu et approuvé, paraphe**

signification (*nf*) notification (of a judgement, etc.). *See* **avis**

situation (*nf*) *see* **irrégulier, régulier**

SMIC (*nm*) the minimum hourly rate of pay which all employers must respect. The initials stand for **salaire**

minimum de croissance. *See* **tarif syndical**

SNALC *see* **Syndicat National des Lycées et Collèges**

SNCF (*nf*) the French railways. *See* **Société Nationale des Chemins de Fer**

SNES *see* **Syndicat National des Enseignants du Second Degré Classique, Moderne et Technique**

SNESup *see* **Syndicat National de l'Enseignement Supérieur**

société anonyme (SA) a limited company. This is usually a larger institution, in particular larger than one taking the status of an **SARL**. The **SA** offers shares to the general public. The minimum number of shareholders is laid down by law, and they are liable for the company's debts only up to the value of their shares. *See below*

société anonyme à responsabilité limitée (SARL) (*nf*) a status usually taken by medium-sized companies. A number of associates, whose minimum number is two and maximum number is fifty, each contribute a capital sum, the minimum amount of which is laid down by law. The associates are liable for the company's debts only up to the amount they have contributed. This type of company does not offer shares to the public. *See above*

Société Générale (*nf*) one of France's largest national banks

Société Immobilière pour le Commerce et l'Industrie (SICOMI) (*nf*) an establishment providing loans for the leasing and buying of business premises, usually in the form of **crédit bail**

Société Nationale des Chemins de Fer (SNCF) (*nf*) the French national railway, usually known by its initials

solde (*nm*) (1) a sale, sales (in a shop)   (2) a balance, an amount still left to pay, balance outstanding (on an account). *See below*

solde créditeur (*nm*) credit balance, amount in the black

solde débiteur (*nm*) debit balance, amount in the red. *See* **compte créditeur**

solde de tout compte (*nm*) a letter or certificate issued by an employer to a departing employee, confirming that all financial matters are settled

solder (se . . .) (*vb*) to end in, show. **les comptes se soldaient par un déficit** the accounts showed a loss

SOS Amitié (*nm*) a Samaritans-style telephone helpline

SOS Racisme (*nm*) an organization set up to fight racism in France. Its Paris telephone number is (00-33-1) 42-05-44-44.

souche (*nf*) (1) a counterfoil, stub. **carnet à souches** a counterfoil book (2) a chimney-stack

sous-bail (*nm*) a sublease, subletting. *Same as* **sous-location**

sous-baux (*nm.pl*) *plural of* **sous-bail**

sous-cité (*adj*) below-mentioned

sous-évaluation (*nf*) undervaluation, underestimation (of the value of a property, etc.)

sous-évaluer (*vb*) to undervalue, underestimate the price of

sous-indiqué (*adj*) below-mentioned

sous-location (*nf*) a sublease, subletting. A lease renting out a property, given not by the owner of the property, but by one of the tenants, who is already renting it from the owner. *Same as* **sous-bail**. *See* **location**

sous-louer (*vb*) to sublet. *See above*

sous-préfet (*nm*) the official directly under and responsible to a **préfet**. The **sous-préfet** is a **fonctionnaire** and based in his or her own **sous-préfecture**.

sous-seing privé (*nm*) see **acte sous-seing privé**

sous-traitant (*nm*) a subcontractor. *See below*

sous-traité (*nm*) a subcontract

sous-traiter (*vb*) (1) to subcontract, to farm out work, in a situation in which a person who has signed a contract to carry out a task gives to someone else a contract to carry out a part (or sometimes the whole) of the task (2) to become a subcontractor, to enter into an agreement to carry out subcontract work   (3) to sublet (a property). *See* **sous-location**

stage (*nm*) (1) a training period   (2) a training course. *See* **formation**

standing (*nm*) standing, luxury. **immeuble de standing** a block of luxury flats

statuer (*vb*) to give a formal judgement or ruling on (in a court case, etc.). **sursis à statuer** a postponement or deferment of a court judgement. *See* **sursis**

statut (*nm*) (1) a rule, regulation, statute   (2) status. **le statut de salarié** the status of employee

studio (*nm*) a one-bedroom flat, bedsit. *See* **agence immobilière, pièce**

subvention (*nf*) a grant, subsidy

    subvention pour la lutte contre l'insalubrité (*nf*) a home-improvement grant paid to the owners of sub-standard accommodation, which must be repaid if the occupier moves out within fifteen years. *See* **prime à l'amélioration de l'habitat**

succession (*nf*) (1) succession   (2) an estate, inheritance. **partager une succession** to share in an inheritance. **par voie de succession** by right of succession. *See* **droits de succession**

sur-cité (*adj*) above-mentioned

sur-indiqué (*adj*) above-mentioned

surenchère (*nf*) an overbid, a higher bid. In property sales by auction, other bidders have ten days *after* the auction has ended in which to lodge a new bid of at least 10 per cent above the agreed selling price. **faire une surenchère (sur)** *same as* **surenchérir**

surenchérir (*v.int*) to put in a higher bid, to raise one's bid

surnom (*nm*) (a false friend) a nickname. 'Surname' is either **nom de famille** or simply **nom**

sursis (*nm*) (1) a reprieve (2) suspension. **peine avec sursis** a suspended sentence (3) deferment, postponement (of call-up for national service, etc.)

suspensif/ive (*adj*) a **clause suspensive** is a clause written into a contract – such as a buying agreement or employment contract – which stipulates certain conditions which, if not met, allow the contract to be cancelled

suspicion légitime (*nf*) lack of impartiality. People involved in a court or industrial tribunal action can ask for the case to be transferred to another court if they have reason to doubt the impartiality of the judges, for example, because of excessive familiarity with, or prior knowledge of, the opposing party.

synallagmatique (*adj*) *see* **contrat synallagmatique**

syndic (*nm*) a legally appointed receiver

syndic d'immeuble (*nm*) the manager of a block of flats. *See* **conseil syndical**, **gérant**

syndicat (*nm*) (1) a (trade) union (2) a syndicate (3) an association. *See below*

    syndicat d'initiative (*nm*) a tourist information office

    syndicat de propriétaires (*nm*) a landlords' association

    Syndicat Général de l'Education Nationale (SGEN) (*nm*) a major union for teachers and others working in education

    syndicat interdépartemental (*nm*) an association of regional authorities

    Syndicat National de l'Enseignement Supérieur (SNESup) (*nm*) a small but influential union of around 5,000 teachers in higher education

    Syndicat National des Enseignants du Second Degré Classique, Moderne et Technique (SNES) (*nm*) a large union for teachers in secondary education (**collège**, **lycée**), with around 70,000 members

    Syndicat National des Lycées et Collèges (SNALC) (*nm*) a moderate union for teachers in secondary education

syndicat ouvrier (*nm*) a trade union

syndicat patronal (*nm*) a federation of employers, an employers' organization

système D (*nm*) getting by, sorting things out for yourself, being resourceful. **D** here stands for **débrouillard**, smart, canny, resourceful. *Système D* is the name of a popular do-it-yourself magazine. **Système D** is also a controversial issue in the red-tape-bound French society. It refers to the attempt by individuals to do things their own way instead of following correct procedure, but has two separate meanings. The first is a helpful and sensible attempt to save time by cutting through unnecessary paperwork and formalities. The second is the breaking of rules from antisocial motives. *See* **piston**

T

tabac (*nm*) a specially licensed shop, marked with a red cigar above the door, which usually occupies one corner of a bar, and sells tobacco and cigarettes. It also sells stamps and telephone cards. *See* **télécarte, timbre**

tarif (*nm*) (1) a price-list (2) a tariff. *See* **barème, frais, honoraires**

tarif EJP (*nm*) an off-peak electricity charge offered by the Electricity Board (**Electricité de France**)

tarif postal (*nm*) postal charges or rates

tarif syndical (*nm*) the union rate, the going rate (for doing a job). *See* **SMIC**

tarifs douaniers (*nm.pl*) customs charges. *See* **impôt**

taxe (*nf*) tax. This can refer to income tax, as in **taxe sur le revenu**, but is more often used in the sense of a tax narrower in scope than an **impôt**, which is imposed on certain kinds of official service such as the issuing of marriage certificates. *See below and* **franchise, impôt, tarif, timbre**

taxe d'habitation (*nf*) the rates, council tax. A local tax paid by the occupants of a property – who are not necessarily the owners – based on its value, and forming part of the local taxes, **impôts locaux**. *See* **taxe foncière**

taxe foncière (*nf*) a property tax payable by *owners* on each of their properties. This is not paid by tenants who pay instead the **taxe d'habitation**.

taxe piscicole (*nf*) a fishing tax, paid by anglers where fishing permits are required

taxe professionnelle (*nf*) a local tax paid by those who earn their living from fees rather than a fixed salary. *See* **barème, honoraires**

taxe sur la valeur ajoutée (TVA) (*nf*) value-added tax

téléachat (*nm*) shopping by television, using either telephone or **télétel**

télécarte (*nf*) a telephone card for use in public phone boxes, obtainable from a post office or **tabac**

télécopie (*nf*) fax. The word **fax** (*nm*) is common.

télétel (*nm*) a form of teletext service, which offers a vast range of services to those who are connected to the **minitel** system

temporaire (*adj*) temporary. *See* **agence de placement, contrat de travail à durée déterminée, intérimaire, travail**

terrain (*nm*) (1) ground, terrain   (2) a sports pitch, ground, court, course (golf)   (3) a plot of land. **terrain à bâtir** a building plot. **terrain à lotir** land for dividing into plots. *See* **constructible, lot, lotissement, plan d'occupation des sols, restaurer, viabilisé**

testament (*nm*) a will, last will and testament. *See below and* **administrateur, communauté, donation-partage, exécuteur, patrimoine, succession**

testament authentique (*nm*) a will drawn up formally by a solicitor in the presence of witnesses. *Also known as* **testament par acte public**. *See below and* **acte, notaire**

testament mystique (*nm*) a will, handwritten by the testator, then placed in a sealed envelope and handed to a solicitor in the presence of witnesses

TGV *see* **Train à Grande Vitesse**

ticket modérateur (*nm*) that part of the cost of a prescription for medicines which patients must pay themselves, because it is not covered by a national, private or job-related medical insurance. The amount can vary from around 2 to 25 per cent, with Social Security paying a guaranteed 75 per cent and the rest topped up by private or occupational insurance. **exonération de ticket modérateur** (*nf*) a form given by a doctor which exempts certain categories of people, such as those with long-term illnesses, from having to pay this extra amount. *See* **assurance maladie, bon de docteur, vignette**

ticket-repas (*nm*) *see* **ticket-restaurant**

ticket-restaurant (*nm*) a luncheon voucher. *Also known as* **ticket-repas** or **titre-restaurant**

tierce (*adj*) *feminine of* **tiers**

tiercé (*nm*) the tote. Nationally organized horse-race betting

tiers/tierce) (*adj*) third, in the legal sense of a third party or independent party. **tierce opposition** (*nf*) a legal appeal, against a judgement made in court, by a third party. This person must not be personally involved in the dispute or the court proceedings, but lodges the appeal on the grounds that his or her interests might be damaged by the court's judgement. *See below*

tiers (*nm*) a third party, third person (in law). **attestation d'un tiers** (*nf*) a statement made by a third party, an independent person, an outsider, or someone not directly involved in the matter under discussion. *See* **tierce opposition**

timbre (*nm*) (1) a postage stamp (2) an official duty stamp (3) a penalty stamp; a **timbre amende** is a way of paying a fixed penalty (**amende forfaitaire**), such as a parking ticket, and can be bought at a post office or **tabac**. *See below and* **majoré, sanction administrative**

timbre fiscal (nm) an excise stamp

timbre-horadateur (nm) a time and date stamp (from parking meters, etc.)

timbre-quittance (nm) a receipt stamp. *See* **quittance**

timbre-taxe (nm) an excess postage, or pay-on-delivery, stamp. This indicates how much the receiver will have to pay on a letter or parcel sent without full payment by the sender.

titre-restaurant (nm) *see* **ticket-restaurant**

titulaire (nm/f) (1) the holder (of a post)   (2) the holder of a certificate, permit or other accreditation   (3) a person or official legally entitled to carry out a certain act. *See* **autorisation**, **responsable**

Train à Grande Vitesse (TGV) (nm) the high-speed train, which has an average speed of 260 kilometres per hour

traitement (nm) (1) a salary   (2) a (medical) treatment   (3) processing, treating (of an industrial product, etc.)

trampolin (nm) a work scheme for unemployed people run by the **aide sociale**, which advertises hourly-paid odd jobs, like gardening

transcription (nf) a transcript, transcription, copying out, copy (normally in a formal or legal sense of a copy of an official document). *See* **ampliation**, **copie**, **double**

translation (nf) a transfer (of property, rights, etc.), conveyancing. A false friend. The normal word for translation is *traduction*.

Transparences (nf.pl) a very useful and free set of simple guides to aspects of employment law. There are over twenty of these brochures, covering everything from different kinds of work contract to procedures of dismissal. They are available from the **Inspection du Travail** which, unfortunately, will not send them to people living abroad.

travail (nm) work. *See below and* **amplitude journalière**, **ANPE**, **Conseil de Prud'hommes**, **contrat de travail**, **convention collective**, **durée**, **engagement de non-concurrence**, **équivalence**,

Inspection du Travail, intérimaire, licenciement, lieu de travail, précarité, publicité mensongère, temporaire, trampolin

travail à domicile (*nm*) working from home

travail à quart (*nm*) shift work. *See* **roulement**

travail à temps partiel (*nm*) part-time work

travail clandestin (*nm*) undeclared employment, working on the side. As in most things, the French are much stricter on tax evasion than their British counterparts. The consequences of being classed as having a hidden source of income can be as severe as the definition of a second livelihood itself. For example, to sell at more than two car boot sales a year is classed as having a second occupation as a **brocanteur**.

travail de vacances (*nm*) holiday work

travail intermittent (*nm*) occasional work, irregular work. *See* **vacation**

travail saisonnier (*nm*) seasonal work. *See* **vacation**

travail temporaire (*nm*) temporary work, but in the sense of *temping* for a temporary jobs agency (**agence de travail**). A temporary job in the usual English sense is **un poste**, or **un contrat de travail, à durée déterminée**. *See* **contrat de travail, durée, intérimaire, précaire**

travailleur étranger (*nm*) *see* **ouvrier**

tribunal (*nm*) the usual name for a court, tribunal. *See* **cour, crime, juge**

tribunal administratif (*nm*) an administrative court. A tribunal of appeal which people approach who feel that they have been ill-treated by state officials. Its services are free, and the plaintiff must first have exhausted the normal channels of complaint. *See* **bavure**

tribunal correctionnel (*nm*) the branch of the **tribunal de grande instance** (county court) dealing with *criminal* rather than *civil* offences, that is to say, those that fall within the orbit of the **Code Pénal** rather than the **Code Civil**

tribunal d'exception (*nm*) a specialist court dealing usually with the least serious range of offences (**infractions**), which are called **contraventions**. These are usually petty offences punishable by a fine. The **tribunaux d'exception** include:

(1) **tribunal d'instance civile** (*nm*), or in some areas the **tribunal de police** (*nm*), dealing with minor offences such as speeding

(2) **tribunal pour mineurs** or **tribunal pour enfants** (*nm*) a juvenile court. More serious cases involving those over 16 are dealt with by the **cour d'assises des mineurs**.

(3) **tribunal de commerce** (*nm*) a commercial court, staffed by part-time judges drawn from the business community

(4) **tribunal des affaires de Sécurité Sociale** (*nm*) a court dealing with Social Security disputes

(5) **tribunal aux armées** (*nm*) a military court

(6) **tribunal des baux ruraux** (*nm*) a court dealing with disputes over rural and farming tenancies. *Sometimes called the* **tribunal paritaire des baux ruraux**

(7) **Conseil de Prud'hommes** (*nm*) an industrial tribunal. *See* **conciliation, médiation**

tribunal de grande instance (*nm*) the main court of a **département**, and so similar to a British Crown Court. However, it is more like the British High Court in that it deals with cases which are more serious than those a Crown Court would normally address. It is concerned with the second, more serious, level of offence (**infraction**) known as **délits**. It has two arms:

(1) **tribunal de grande instance civile** (*nm*) dealing with civil cases, under the **Code Civil**, such as those involving large amounts of money. It deals also with issues like guardianship. *See* **tutelle**

(2) **tribunal correctionnel** (*nm*) dealing with criminal cases under the **Code Pénal**

tribunal d'instance (*nm*) a magistrates' court

tribunal de police (*nm*) a criminal court, operating in some areas instead of a **tribunal d'instance civile**, and dealing with **infractions**. *See* **tribunal d'exception**

tribunal de première instance (*nm*) the court of first instance. This title covers the first two categories of French court, the **tribunal d'instance** and the **tribunal de grande instance**, which deal with **contraventions** and **délits**, as distinct from the higher courts or **cours**, which deal with **crimes**. *See* **infraction**

tribunal des conflits (*nm*) one of the country's highest courts, adjudicating on matters of State policy

tribunal paritaire des baux ruraux (*nm*) *see* **tribunal des baux ruraux**

tribunaux des flagrants délits (flags) (*nm.pl*) A person caught red-handed (**en flagrant délit**) in the act of committing a crime, whether a **délit** or an **infraction**, is bought directly before the **Procureur de la République**, who can order an appearance before a judge in the appropriate tribunal within five days. The aim is to simplify and speed up the trial of people whose guilt is not in doubt.

trois jours (*nm.pl*) the selection board for national service, to which those eligible reported for medical and other tests. *See* **service national**

troisième âge (*nm*) senior citizens, old-age pensioners, retired people. **l'université du troisième âge** the university of the third age, adult education classes for retired people

tronc commun (*nm*) the national curriculum (in secondary education), common syllabus

tutelle (*nf*) guardianship, usually in the sense of a legal ruling passed by a **juge des tutelles** in the **tribunal de grande instance**

TVA (*nf*) VAT (**taxe sur la valeur ajoutée**)

union libre (*nf*) common-law marriage. A couple living together may draw up **une attestation d'union libre**, a certificate affirming that they are living together and are to be considered as man and wife. *See* **communauté, concubinage**

université (*nf*) a university. **université libre** a private university. *See* **cité universitaire, troisième âge**

urbanisme (*nm*) town planning regulations. A document drawn up by the local authorities and made available at the **mairie** for public inspection. It lays out local plans and policy on building and development, explaining what kind of developments are permitted and the details of future developments which may affect other properties. *See* **plan d'occupation des sols**

urne (*nf*) a ballot-box, election, poll. **aller aux urnes** to vote, to go to the polls

usufruit (*nm*) usufruct. The right of one person to have use of the belongings of another, or to dispose of the produce of that item, without having the right of ownership of the item itself, for example, the right of a tenant to eat the apples growing on a tree in the garden of a rented house

utilité publique (*nf*) an organization, charity or product which is officially recognized as being in the public interest, for example, Perrier mineral water. This status creates tax benefits.

vacataire (*nm/f*) someone who is employed by the State on an irregular basis (i.e. a **non-titulaire**), working a certain number of hours or sessions (**vacations**). *See below*

vacation (*nf*) (a false friend) a work session. The legal status of these is unclear, as the **Code du Travail** makes no mention of them. In principle, they are a form of employment used by the Civil Service, in which people are called in for hours of work as and when needed. However, they have latterly been used by other employers, such as schools of English recruiting foreign teachers. This has put them at the centre of controversy. They guarantee neither work nor income, meaning that the 'employee' could be left without income for six months, yet still not be able to claim benefits or work elsewhere. Not to be confused with holiday work, which is **travail saisonnier** or **travail de vacances**. *See* **contrat, dol, engagement de non-concurrence, travail**

validité (*nf*) validity. **un permis de conduire en cours de validité** a current driving licence

VD a false friend. It stands not for what you would expect (which is **maladie vénérienne**) but for a type of registered mail. *See* **envoi en valeur déclarée, lettre recommandée**

vénérien/enne (*adj*) **maladie vénérienne** VD. *See above*

vente à crédit (*nf*) *see* **crédit**

vente aux enchères (*nf*) an auction. *See* **commissaire-priseur, dépôt de vente, salle des ventes**

vente en viager (*nf*) *same as* **rente viagère**. *See* **viager**

vente judiciaire (*nf*) the official selling off of bankrupt or confiscated stock. *See* **astreinte, emprise**

versement (*nm*) (1) payment (of wages, etc.). **versement par chèque** payment by cheque (2) an instalment (of a fee, etc.). *See* **traitement**

Verts (Les) (*nm.pl*) the Green Party, Ecology Party

veuillez (*vb*) please. **veuillez agréer, Monsieur/Madame, l'expression de mes sentiments distingués** yours faithfully. Letter-writing in France is taken seriously, with elaborate formulae of address. *See* **courrier, Me., parvenir**

viabilisé/e (*adj*) with services (laid on). **terrain viabilisé** a plot of land with water, sewage and gas or electric services laid on

viager/ère (*adj*) **à titre viager** for life, for the duration of one's life. *See* **rente viagère, secours viager**

vice (*nm*) (1) vice, wickedness, perversion (2) a fault, flaw, irregularity, defect. **vices de consentement** lack of proper consent, obtaining consent by unlawful means, an irregularity in an agreement between two parties, making their contract invalid. *See* **caduc, contrat, dol**

vidéoposte (*nm*) a teletext service for bank account holders, which allows them to check their accounts and carry out a range of transactions by **minitel**

vignette (*nf*) (1) a road-tax disc (on a car) (2) one of the removable labels on medicines which have to be unpeeled and stuck on to a special form (**feuille de soins**) in order to claim a refund from the Social Services. *See* **assurance maladie**

virement bancaire (*nm*) a credit transfer, transfer of cash by bank order. **faire un virement** to make a credit transfer

virement postal (*nm*) a giro transfer. *See* **mandat-poste**

visa de long séjour (*nm*) a residence permit for up to three months, required by nationals from outside the European Union. *See* **carte de séjour, permis de travail**

voies de fait (*nf.pl*) assault. **se livrer à des voies de fait sur qn** to assault someone. *See* **blessure par imprudence**

volet (*nm*) a section of an official form or document. **volet de facturation** the invoice section of a document

volontaires du service national (VSN) (*nm.pl*) national service volunteers; people who volunteered for an extended period of national service (**service national**) in return for improved pay and conditions. *See* **préparation militaire, service national**

vote par procuration (*nf*) a proxy vote, asking someone else to cast your vote for you, an arrangement which must be made in front of a solicitor or other recognized public official

VSN *see* **volontaires du service national**

Z

ZAD *see* **zone d'aménagement différé**

zone à régime préférentiel (*nf*) a business enterprise zone. An area designated for redevelopment, offering grants and tax incentives to businesses which set up there. *See* **zone franche**

zone d'aménagement différé (ZAD) (*nf*) a form of compulsory purchase area, in which the authorities have the first option to buy any buildings or land that come up for sale, over a period of up to fourteen years

zone franche (*nf*) a reduced-tax zone, usually part of a business enterprise zone aimed at attracting businesses to an area. *See* **zone à régime préférentiel**

List of Entries by Subject

In order to facilitate study, terms contained in the dictionary are listed below by subject matter. Terms marked with an asterisk indicate areas of special difficulty or importance, mostly connected with employment. In the author's view, it is essential that anyone thinking of moving to France should be aware of these and, where necessary, seek professional advice on them.

Banking and Business

(For more details on the workplace see **Employment**; for details on contracts and solicitors, see **Law, Police and Solicitors**.)

accise, acompte, action, action au porteur, action libérée, action ordinaire, action privilégiée, actionnaire, adjudication, Administration des Douanes, Administration des Impôts, agence, agence commerciale, agence comptable, agence d'assurance, agence fiscale accréditée, agence maritime, agent, agent commercial, agent comptable, agent d'affaires, agent de fisc, agréé par l'Etat, amnistie fiscale, année fiscale, apurement, ASSEDIC, assiette, associé, autogestion, avoir fiscal

bail, bailleur, banque d'affaires, banque de consignation, banque de crédit, banque de dépôt, baux commerciaux, biens d'équipement, biens et services, biens immobiliers, biens immeublés, biens meublés, biens mobiliers, bilan, billet de commerce, billet d'ordre, bon, bon de caisse, bon de commande, bon d'épargne, bon de garantie, bon de livraison, bon du trésor, bon pour accord, bordereau d'achat, bordereau d'envoi, bordereau de livraison, bordereau de salaire, bordereau de vente, bordereau de versement, brut, bulletin, bulletin de perception, Bureau de Vérification de la Publicité (BVP)

CAC 40, cadre, caisse, Caisse d'Epargne et de Prévoyance,

Caisse Nationale d'Epargne, Caisse Nationale de Prévoyance, capital, capital circulant, capital d'exploitation, capital fixe, capital risque, capital social, carence, carnet à souches, carnet de chèques, carnet de commande, carte d'identité, CEDEX, centre d'information civique (CIC), cessation d'activité, cession-bail, cession de parts, CGPME, chambre de commerce et d'industrie, charges, charges d'exploitation, charges financières, charges locatives, charges sociales, chèque, chèque au porteur, chèque barré, chèque certifié, chèque de banque, chèque de voyage, chèque en blanc, chèque non-barré, chèque-repas, chèque sans provision, chèque-vacances, chéquier, CIDEX, CIO, cité, client, clôture, CNP, CNPF, Code du Travail, Code de Commerce, Code de Procédure Civile, Code des Sociétés, CODEVI, compensable, comptabilité, comptable, compte, compte à terme, compte bancaire, compte bloqué, compte chèques postaux, compte courant, compte créditeur, compte de dépôts, compte épargne-logement, compte odysée, Compte pour le Développement Industriel, compte sur livret, concessionnaire, conciliateur, concurrence, Confédération Générale des Petites et Moyennes Entreprises, conseil, conseil d'administration, consentir un prêt, constat, contracter un emprunt, contrat de fonction, contrat de réservation, créancier, création d'une société, crédit, Crédit Agricole, crédit bail, crédit bancaire, crédit documentaire, Crédit du Nord, Crédit Foncier, crédit hypothécaire, Crédit Lyonnais, crédit municipal, Crédit Mutuel, créditeur, créer une société

débiteur, déclaration de faillite, déclaration d'impôts, déclaration de ressources, déclaration de revenus, dégrèvement, délai de livraison, délai de réflexion, délai de rigueur, demande d'immatriculation au registre du commerce, dépens en capital, déposer les comptes, dépôt des comptes, Direction Départementale de la Concurrence, de la Consommation et de la Répression des Fraudes, Directoire, dissoudre une société, document comptable, domicilier une société, droit des affaires, droit des sociétés, droit fiscal, droits de mutation, droits de reproduction

emprunt, emprunt-logement, emprunteur, endossement, endosser un chèque, engagement, enregistrer, équipement industriel, expert-comptable, expertiser, exploitation, exploitation commerciale facture, faillite, faire faillite, fermeture annuelle, fête légale, feuille d'impôt, fichier, fisc, fonds de commerce, fonds de roulement, forfait, formation, foyer fiscal, frais généraux, franchise, franchisé, fraude

garantie, garantie légale, gérant, guichet

hors taxe

immatriculation, immatriculé, imposition, impôt, impôt de solidarité sur la fortune, impôt local, impôt sur le revenu, irrégulier

jour de congé, jour de fête, jour férié, jour ouvrable

lettre recommandée

majoration, majoré, mandat-lettre, mandat-poste, mise de fonds, moratoire

nom de marque, non-concurrence

orientation

patron, patronal, patronat, percepteur, perception, péréquation, personne morale, piston, plan, plus-value, postéclair, pouvoir, prélèvement, prêt, prêt patronal, prime, promesse de vente, propriétaire, publicité mensongère

quittance

rallonge, rapporter, ratification, ratification de vente, recouvrement, registre de comptabilité, régler, relevé bancaire, relevé de compte, relevé d'identité bancaire, répondant, responsable

SA, salariat, solde, solde créditeur, solde débiteur, solde de tout compte, se solder, souche, stage, surenchère, synallagmatique

tarif, tarif postal, tarifs douaniers, taxe, taxe foncière, taxe professionnelle, taxe sur la valeur ajoutée (TVA), ticket-restaurant, timbre-quittance, titre-restaurant, traitement, travail clandestin, TVA

urbanisme, usufruit, utilité publique

vente à crédit, vidéoposte

ZAD, zone à régime préférentiel, zone d'aménagement différé, zone franche

Education

administration, agrégation, allocation d'éducation spécialisée, allocation rentrée scolaire, année scolaire, association de parents d'elèves, association sportive scolaire, assurance scolaire, auxiliaire (maître auxiliaire)

baccalauréat, baccalauréat international, bachelier, BELC, BEP, bibliobus, bibliothèque centrale de prêt, bibliothèque municipale, Bibliothèque Nationale (BN), Bibliothèque Publique d'Information, bourse d'enseignement secondaire, bourse d'enseignement supérieur, bourse d'études, brevet, brevet d'apprentissage, Brevet d'Etudes Professionnelles, bulletin, bulletin trimestriel, Bureau pour l'Enseignement de la Langue et de la Civilisation (BELC)

cantine, CAP, CAPE, CAPES, CAPET, CAPLP, carnet, carnet de notes, carte d'étudiant, carte de lecteur, CEC, centre aéré, centre d'action culturelle, centre de documentation et d'information (CDI), centre de formation d'apprentis (CFA), centre d'information et de documentation jeunesse (CIDJ), centre d'information et d'orientation (CIO), centre de loisirs sans hébergement (CLSH), Centre de Recherches et d'Etudes pour la Diffusion du Français (CREDIF), centre de vacances et de loisirs, Centre International d'Etudes Pédagogiques (CIEP), centre international des étudiants et stagiaires (CIES), Centre National d'Enseignement à Distance (CNED), CEP, certificat d'études primaires, certificat d'immatriculation, certificat de scolarité, cité universitaire, classe, classe de neige, coefficient familial, collège, colonie de vacances, concours, concours externe, concours général, concours interne, congé d'enseignement et de recherche, congé de formation, congé parental d'éducation, congé sabbatique, conseil de classe, conseil des maîtres, conseil des professeurs, conseiller d'éducation, conseiller d'orientation, cycle d'observation

délégué-élèves, dépenses scolaires, Diplôme d'Etudes Supérieures Spécialisées (DESS), Diplôme d'Etudes Universitaires de Sciences et Techniques (DEUST), Diplôme d'Etudes Universitaires Générales (DEUG), Diplôme Universitaire de Technologie (DUT), doctorat école, Ecole Centrale de Lyon, Ecole Centrale de Paris, école libre, école maternelle, Ecole Nationale d'Administration (ENA), Ecole Nationale d'Ingénieurs (ENI), Ecole Nationale d'Ingénieurs de Travaux Agricoles (ENITA), Ecole Nationale Supérieure Agronomique (ENSA), Ecole Nationale Supérieure d'Arts et Métiers (ENSAM), Ecole Nationale Supérieure des Arts Décoratifs (ENSAD), Ecole Nationale Supérieure des Beaux-Arts (ENSBA), Ecole Normale Supérieure (ENS), école primaire, ENA, énarque, ENI, ENITA, ENS, ENSA, ENSAD, ENSAM, ENSBA, enseignement, *équivalence

formation, formation complémentaire, formation continue, formation professionnelle, frais de scolarité

garde champêtre

halte-garderie

instituteur, internat, interne

licence, licencié, lycée

maison de la culture, maîtrise, mastère, maternelle

Office National d'Information sur les Enseignements et les Professions

patrimoine, pension, pension alimentaire, premier cycle, professeur, professeur agrégé, professeur certifié, proviseur

ramassage scolaire, rectorat, redoublement, rentrée, répondant

scolaire, scolarisation, scolariser, scolarité, Section d'Education Spécialisée (SES), SGEN, SNALC, SNES, stage, Syndicat Général de l'Education Nationale (SGEN), Syndicat National de l'Enseignement Supérieur (SNESup), Syndicat National des Enseignants du Second Degré Classique, Moderne et Technique, Syndicat National des Lycées et Collèges (SNALC)

tronc commun

université, université libre

Employment

(*Also see* **Banking and Business**)

abusif, accord collectif, accroissement temporaire d'activité, actifs, agence de placement, Agence Nationale pour l'Amélioration des Conditions d'Emploi, Agence Nationale pour l'Emploi (ANPE), AGIRC, allocation de base, allocation de chômage, allocation de fin de droit, allocation de garde de famille à domicile, allocation de salaire unique, allocation pour frais de garde, amélioration des conditions du travail (Agence Nationale pour l'Amélioration des Conditions du Travail), amiable compositeur, ampliation, *amplitude journalière, ancienneté, annexe, *ANPE, à pourvoir, APEC, *AR, *arbitrage, ARRCO, arrêt de travail, ASSEDIC, assiduité, assiette, assimilé, Association des Régimes de Retraites Complémentaires (ARRCO), Association Générale des Institutions de Retraite des Cadres (AGIRC), Association pour l'Emploi dans l'Industrie et le Commerce (ASSEDIC), Association pour l'Emploi des Cadres (APEC), associé, assurance accident du travail, assurance chômage, assurance invalidité, assurance maladie, assurance maternité, assurance personnelle, assurance vieillesse, assurance volontaire, assurances sociales, assuré social, atelier protégé, attestation, attestation de travail, autogestion, avancement, avantages en nature nourriture et logement, avenant

BAS, BEP, bon pour accord, brevet, Brevet d'Etudes Professionnelles (BEP), Bureau de l'Aide Sociale (BAS)

cadre, caisse de la Sécurité Sociale, cantine, CAP, centre de formation d'apprentis (CFA), centre d'information et d'orientation (CIO), Certificat d'Aptitude Professionnelle (CAP), certificat de travail, CFDT, CFTC, CGC, CGPME, CGT, charges sociales, chèque-repas, chèque-restaurant, chèque-vacances, chômage, chômeur, CIO, cité administrative, *clandestin, *clause suspensive, Code du Travail, Code de la Sécurité Sociale, collaborateur, comité d'entreprise, comité d'hygiène, de sécurité et des conditions de travail (CHSCT), commission d'arbitrage, *commission de conciliation, Commission Technique d'Orientation et de Reclassement Professionnel (COTOREP), compositeur, comptabilité, comptabilité des sociétés, comptable, conciliateur, conciliation, *concours, concours externe, concours interne, concours de la Fonction Publique, concours général, concurrence, Confédération Française Démocratique du Travail (CFDT), Confédération Française des Travailleurs Chrétiens (CFTC), Confédération Générale des Cadres (CGC), Confédération Générale des Petites et Moyennes Entreprises (CGPME), Confédération Générale du Travail (CGT), congé, congé annuel, congé d'enseignement et de recherche, congé de formation, congé de maladie, congé de maternité, congé parental d'éducation, congé sabbatique, conseil, *Conseil de Prud'hommes, contractuels, *contrat de travail à durée déterminée, *contrat de travail à durée indéterminée, *contrat verbal, contribuable, *convention collective, copie certifiée conforme, cotisation, COTOREP, crèche

déclaration de revenus, délai-congé, délai de préavis, délégué de site, délégué du personnel, demande d'emploi, démarchage, direction, Direction Départementale du Travail et de l'Emploi, directoire, disponible au travail, double, droit de grève, droit de retrait, droit syndical, durée, *durée hebdomadaire maximum du travail, *durée quotidienne maximum du travail

*économique, effectif, employé, *engagement de non-concurrence, entretien, *équivalence, *éventuel, expédition

fédération d'industrie, fermeture annuelle, fête légale, feuille, feuille d'impôt, feuille de maladie, feuille de paie, feuille de présence, fiche, fiche de paie, fiche de soins, fisc, fixation, fonction publique, fonctionnaire, Force Ouvrière, formation, formation complémentaire, formation continue, formation professionnelle, formulaire, foyer des jeunes travailleurs, foyer fiscal

grief

*harcèlement sexuel, heures supplémentaires

immatriculation, imposition (avis d'), impôt sur le revenu, inspecteur du travail, Inspection du Travail, intérimaire, irrégulier

jour de congé, jour de fête, jour férié, jour ouvrable, jurisconsulte *lettre recommandée, *licenciement, *licenciement abusif, *licenciement sans cause réelle ou sérieuse, licencier, *lieu de travail

*maison de l'avocat, mise en garde

*non-concurrence, non-titulaire

Office National d'Information sur les Enseignements et les Professions, orientation

patron, patronal, patronat, pension de retraite, percepteur, perception, péréquation, permanent, piston, plainte, précaire, précarité, prélèvement, prestation en nature, prêt patronal, prétensions, *prime de précarité, publicité mensongère

régime, régimes d'assurance vieillesse, registre de comptabilité, réglementation de travail, *renouvellement, *renvoi, répondant, responsable, retraite, *rétrogradation, revenu minimum d'insertion (RMI), roulement

salaire minimum de croissance (SMIC), salaire de référence, salariat, section, Sécurité Sociale, semaine légale, SMIC, stage, *suspensif, syndicat, Syndicat Général de l'Education Nationale (SGEN), Syndicat National des Enseignants du Second Degré Classique, Moderne et Technique, Syndicat National des Lycées et Collèges (SNALC), syndicat ouvrier, syndicat patronal, *système D

tarif syndical, taxe, taxe professionnelle, ticket-restaurant, titulaire, trampolin, *Transparences, travail à domicile, travail à quart, *travail clandestin, *travail intermittent, travail saisonnier, *travail temporaire, *travail à temps partiel, tribunal des affaires de Sécurité Sociale

vacataire, *vacation

Family Life, Marriage, Travel

(*Also see* **Social Services**)

abonné, abonnement, accuser réception, achat à crédit, acquéreur, acte de l'état civil, acte de mariage, agence de renseignements, agence matrimoniale, aide personnalisée au logement (APL), aliments, amiable, APL, atteintes à la vie privée, avis d'imposition, avis de signification, avoir

biens, biens communs, biens corporels, biens meublés, biens mobiliers, BIJE, billet international pour les jeunes (BIJE), bon de garantie, bureau de l'état civil

carnet de famille, carte, carte améthyste, carte bleue, carte Carrissimo, carte couple, carte de crédit, carte d'électeur, carte d'étudiant, carte d'identité, carte de lecteur, carte de résident, carte émeraude, carte kiwi, carte nationale d'identité, carte pastel, célibataire, centre aéré, centre de loisirs, centre d'information civique (CIC), centre d'information et de documentation de jeunesse (CIDJ), centre d'information et d'orientation (CIO), certificat de perte, chef de famille, chèque-vacances, CIDJ, CIO, cité administrative, code de la route, communauté, communauté d'acquêts, communauté de la séparation des biens, communauté de meubles et d'acquêts, communauté entre époux, communauté légale, communauté réduite aux acquêts, communauté universelle, concubinage, conditions de ressources, conduite accompagnée, conjoint, conseil de famille, conseiller matrimonial, coordonnées

déclaration de changement de domicile, déclaration d'impôts, déclaration de naissance, déclaration de perte, déclaration de ressources, déclaration de revenus, dégrèvement, délai de réflexion, délit de fuite, demande en divorce, démarchage, déménagement, demeure, dépôt d'ordures, dépôt de vente, destinataire, Direction Départementale de l'Equipement, dispense de bans, divorce, domicile, donation entre époux, donation-partage, droit de la famille, droit de visite, droit social, droits civils, droits civiques, droits dérivés, droits de succession

émancipation, envoi contre remboursement, envoi en valeur déclarée, état civil, extrait d'acte de mariage

familial, fisc

impôt local, impôt sur le revenu, irrégulier

juge aux affaires familiales, juge des enfants

lettre recommandée, levée, liste électorale, livret de famille maison de l'avocat, maison des jeunes et de la culture, maison maternelle, majeur, majoration, majorité, mandat-carte, mandat-lettre, mandat-poste, mariage, mariage civil, mariage religieux, maternité

nationalité, nom et prénom, nom de baptême, nom de famille, nom de femme mariée, nom de jeune fille, numéro vert

officier de l'état civil

percepteur, perception, permis de conduire, petit nom, pharmacie de garde, poste restante, postéclair, prévention routière, PTT

redevance, régime matrimonial, registre de l'état civil, résidence

séparation de corps, séparation des biens, service militaire, service national, SOS Amitié, SOS Racisme

tarif EJP, tarif postal, téléachat, télécarte, télétel

union libre

vénérien

Law, Police and Solicitors

accusation, accusé, acte, acte authentique, acte d'achat, acte d'acquisition, acte de notoriété, acte de vente, acte notarié, acte solennel, acte sous-seing privé, acte sur papier timbré, action civile, action en diffamation, action en justice, actionner, adversaire, affaire, affaire-test, aide judiciaire, aide légale, ajournement, ajourner, alcool au volant, alcootest/alcooltest, aliments, alinéa, aller en justice, amende, amiable, amiable compositeur, ampliation, appel, appelant, appeler, AR, arbitrage, arrêt, arrêté, arrêté ministériel, arrêté municipal, arrêté préfectoral, arrhes, assignation, assigné, assigner qn, assises, astreinte, atteintes à la vie privée, attestation, attestation d'acquisition, audience, audition, autorisation, avenant, avenir, aveu, avis, avocat, avoir, avoué

barème, barreau, bâtonnier, baux commerciaux, baux d'habitation, bavure, biens communs, biens corporels, biens immeublés, biens immobiliers, biens incorporels, biens meublés, biens mobiliers, billet de commerce, blâme, blessure par imprudence, bon pour accord, brigade des moeurs, bureau de conciliation, bureau de jugement, bureau de l'état civil, Bureau de Vérification de la Publicité (BVP)

cabinet, cadre, caduc, caducité, carence, carte d'identité, cas, casier judiciaire, cassation, cause, caution, céans, certificat de perte, chambre civile, chambre correctionnelle, chambre d'accusation, chambre des mises en accusation, chambre des requêtes, chambre sociale, charges, chef, chef d'inculpation, chefs de la demande, citation, citation à comparaître, citation directe, citation en justice, citer, co-contractant, code, code de déontologie, code de la route, code départemental, Code, Code Administratif, Code Civil, Code de Commerce, Code de Justice Militaire, Code de la Construction et de l'Habitation, Code de l'Environnement, Code de la Nationalité, Code de la Santé Publique, de la Famille et de l'Aide Sociale, Code de la Sécurité Sociale, Code de la Mutualité, Code de Procédure Pénale, Code de Procédure Civile, Code de l'Urbanisme, Code des Loyers et de la Copropriété, Code des Sociétés, Code du Travail, Code Electoral, Code Forestier, Code Général des Impôts, Code Pénal, Code Rural, commissaire du gouvernement, commission d'arbitrage, commission de conciliation, commission d'office, commission rogatoire, communication, Compagnies Républicaines de Sécurité (CRS), comparaître, comparution, compétence, compositeur, compromis de vente, conciliateur, conciliation, conclusions, conditions de ressources, conseiller juridique, consentement, constat, contentieux, contradictoire, contraignant, contrainte, contrat, contrat de réservation, contrat verbal, contravention, contrefaçon, contrefaire, contrôle d'identité, convocation, copie certifiée conforme, correctionnel, cosignataire, coupable, Cour, cour de cassation, cour d'appel, cour d'assises, crime

débats, débouter, déclaration, déclaration de non-condamnation, déclaration de perte, déclaration de ressources, dédit, défaut de comparution, défenderesse, défendeur, défense, défenseur, déférer, délictueux, délit, délit de fuite, demande d'aide judiciaire, demande en divorce, demande en justice, demande en renvoi, demande reconventionnelle, déni de justice, dénonciation calomnieuse, dépens, désigné, dispositif, disposition, documents-preuves, dol, domicile, dommages et intérêts, dossier, double, droit, droit civil, droit constitutionnel, droit de chasse, droit de la famille, droit de timbre, droit de visite, droit des affaires, droit des sociétés, droit fiscal, droit international, droit social, droits civils, droits civiques, droits de reproduction, droits dérivés

écrou, émoluments, emprise, enfreindre, engagement, énoncé, enquête, ester en justice, état civil, étude, éventuel, exécuteur, expédition, exploit d'ajournement, exploit d'huissier, expropriation, expulsion de domicile

facultatif, faux témoignage, flags, fondé, force majeure, force obligatoire, forfait, forfaiture, fouille, fourrière, frais, frais d'acte, frais de notaire, frais d'enregistrement, franchise, fraude

gain de cause, garantie légale, garde à vue, garde champêtre, Garde Républicaine, gendarme, Gendarmerie Nationale, greffier, grief

harcèlement sexuel, honoraires, hôtel de police, huissier

inculpé, infraction, injonction de payer, instance, interdiction de séjour, interpellation, interpeller, irrégulier, irrépétible

juge, juge aux affaires familiales, juge-commissaire, juge consulaire, juge de l'application des peines, juge de l'exécution, juge de l'expropriation, juge d'instruction, juge des enfants, juge des loyers, juge des tutelles, juge rapporteur, juge unique, jugement, juré, juridiction, juridictions d'exception, jurisconsulte, jury, justice, justiciable

légitime défense, lettre recommandée, levée, levée de jugement, libération conditionnelle, liberté d'aller et venir, liberté surveillée, litige, loi de 1948, loi Méhaignerie, loi Scrivener

magistrat, magistrat instructeur, maison centrale, maison d'arrêt, maison de correction, maison de l'avocat, maître, majeur, majoration, majoré, majorité, mandat, mandat d'amener, mandat d'arrêt, mandat de comparution, mandat de dépôt, mandat de perquisition, mandataire, mandement, Me., mensonger, mise en accusation

Property and Lodging

achat à crédit, acquéreur, acte, acte authentique, acte d'achat, acte d'acquisition, acte de vente, acte notarié, acte solennel, acte sous-seing privé, acte sur papier timbré, agence immobilière, Agence Nationale pour l'Amélioration de l'Habitat, agent voyer, aide personnalisée au logement (APL), allocation de loyer, allocation logement, ANIL, APL, arrêté, arrêté d'insalubrité, arrêté municipal, arrhes, assurance, assurance automatique acquéreur, assurance incendie, attestation d'acquisition, attestation d'assurance, avenant

bail, bailleur, bâteau, bâtir (terrain à bâtir), baux, baux commerciaux, baux d'habitation, biens meublés, biens mobiliers, bipropriété, bornage

cadastre, cahier des charges, certificat de conformité, cession-bail, changement de résidence, charges, charges locatives, chemin communal, clôture, Code de la Construction et de l'Habitation, Code de l'Urbanisme, Code des Loyers et de la Copropriété, coefficient d'occupation du sol (COS), compromis de vente, concierge, confort acoustique, conseil syndical, consentir un prêt, constat, constructible, CONSUEL, contracter un emprunt, contrat de réservation, copropriété, crédit hypothécaire

déclaration de changement de domicile, déclaration préalable de construction, démembrement de propriété, déménagement, demeure, dépendances, Direction Départementale de l'Equipement, domaine public, domicile, droit de chasse, droit de passage

EDF, emprunt-logement, enregistrement, équipement, équipement électrique d'une maison, état des lieux, expert-foncier, expertiser, exploitation, expulsion de domicile, extrait d'acte de mariage

foncier, fonds de roulement, Fonds National de l'Aide au Logement, foyer, foyer des jeunes travailleurs, frais d'enregistrement

garantie, garantie décennale, garantie de parfait achèvement, géomètre-expert, gérant d'immeuble, gîte

Social Services, Birth, Death, Health, Personal Insurance

acte de baptême, acte de décès, action sanitaire et sociale, Agence Nationale pour l'Amélioration de l'Habitat (ANAH), aide au retour, aide judiciaire, aide légale, aide médicale, aide personnalisée au logement (APL), aide sociale, allocation, allocation assistante maternelle, allocation aux adultes handicapés, allocation aux mères de famille, allocation compensatrice de handicap, allocation de base, allocation de chômage, allocation d'éducation spécialisée, allocation de fin de droit, allocation de garde de famille à domicile, allocation d'insertion, allocation de loyer, allocation de parent isolé, allocation de rentrée scolaire, allocation de salaire unique, allocation de solidarité, allocation des mineurs handicapés, allocation familiale, allocation logement, allocation militaire, allocation pour frais de garde, allocation post-natale, allocation pour jeune enfant, allocation prénatale, allocation spéciale, allocation spéciale vieillesse, allocation supplémentaire du fonds national de solidarité, APL, assiette, assistance, assistance judiciaire, assistance publique, assurance de responsabilité civile, assurance invalidité, assurance maladie, assurance maternité, assurance personnelle, assurance veuvage, assurance vie, assurance vieillesse, assurance volontaire, assuré, assuré social, avis de décès

bail à nourriture, billet de santé, bon de docteur, bulletin de l'état civil, bulletin de naissance, Bureau de l'Aide Sociale (BAS)

caisse d'allocations familiales, caisse de la Sécurité Sociale, capital décès, carnet de maternité, carte de circulation des non-voyants, carte de combattants, carte de famille nombreuse, carte d'invalidité, carte nationale de priorité, carte Paris santé, centre communal d'action sociale, centre d'information civique (CIC), certificat de non-décès, charges familiales, charges sociales, CIC, clinique, coefficient familial, contribuable

décès, déclaration de non-décès, demande d'aide judiciaire, Direction Départementale de l'Action Sanitaire et Sociale (DDASS), dispensaire, dossier médical

étiquette, examen médical prénuptial, exécuteur

famille nombreuse, feuille de maladie, feuille de soins, fiche de soins

hôpital

immatriculation

non-décès

obligation alimentaire, ordonnance

patrimoine, pension alimentaire, pension d'invalidité, pension de retraite, pharmacie de garde, pompes funèbres, pouponnière, prestation, prestation d'invalidité, prestations familiales, prime, prime de transport, radiation, recouvrement par succession

régime complémentaire, régime général, régime matrimonial, régime spécial, régimes d'assurance vieillesse, registre mortuaire

subvention

testament, testament authentique, testament mystique, tutelle

viager, vignette

Index of English Words

The following is *not* a dictionary offering a translation of the English word given, but an *index* directing the reader to the entries dealing with the subject.

building *see* planning permission
building plot *see* plot
business **affaires, fonds de commerce, franchise**
business enterprise zone **ZAD, zone à régime préférentiel, zone franche**

capital **capital, fonds, fortune**
car *see* driving
careers advice **formation, orientation, stage**
certificate **acte, ampliation, attestation, certificat, diplôme, extrait, notoriété**
chamber of commerce **chambre de commerce et d'industrie, chambre des métiers**
cheque **chèque, compensable, virement bancaire**
cheque card **carte bleu, relevé d'identité bancaire**
child allowance **allocation assistante maternelle, allocation d'éducation spécialisée, allocation de garde de famille à domicile, allocation de rentrée scolaire, allocation des mineurs handicapés, allocation familiale, allocation pour frais de garde, allocation pour jeune enfant, allocation prénatale, assurance maternité.** *See* child-minding, single parent's allowance
child-minding **centre aéré, colonie de vacances, crèche, école maternelle, halte-garderie, pouponnière.** *See* child allowance
civil servant **agent titulaire, auxiliaire, employé, fonctionnaire**
Civil Service **l'Administration, cité administrative, fonction publique**
clerk **greffier**
clinic **centre hospitalier, clinique, dispensaire, hôpital**
cohabitation **communauté, concubinage, donation, mariage, union libre**
committee **commission, conseil, délégué, syndic d'immeuble**
common-law marriage **concubinage, union libre**
compensation **dommages et intérêts, indemnité, prime**
competition **concurrence**
conciliation **amiable compositeur, arbitrage, conciliation**
confiscation *see* seizure
contract **acte, compromis de vente, contrat, engagement, promesse de vente**
conurbation **agglomération**
conveyancing *see* house-buying
co-ownership **bipropriété, bornage, copropriété, mitoyennété**
cooling-off period **délai de réflexion**
copy **ampliation, exemplaire, notoriété**
costs **charges, dépens, dommages et intérêts, fonds, frais, irrépétible, mise de fonds**

counterfoil **souche**. *See* receipt

court **chambre, Conseil de Prud'hommes, correctionnel, cour, flags, juge, tribunal**. *See below and* crime

court case **action, affaire, contentieux, instance, justice, litige, procès**. *See above*

crèche *see* child-minding

credit **achat à crédit, crédit, délai de réflexion, emprunt, hypothèque**

credit transfer **virement bancaire**

crime **crime, délit, infraction, quasi-délit**

criminal record **casier judiciaire, déclaration de non-condamnation**

custody **détention, droit de visite, garde à vue, interpellation, prison préventative**

death **acte de décès, décès, état civil, livret de famille, non-décès, pompes funèbres**

deductions **charges sociales, cotisation, prélèvement**

deed **acte, compromis de vente, promesse de vente**. *See* receipt

deed of purchase **acte de vente**. *See* proof of purchase

deferral **renvoi, reporter, sursis**

deregistration **radiation**

dismissal **destitution, licenciement, renvoi, rétrogradation**

distraint *see* seizure

divorce **aliments, conseiller matrimonial, divorce, droit de visite, juge aux affaires familiales**. *See* marriage

doctor **bon de docteur, feuille de soins, vignette**

driving **alcool au volant, alcooltest, assurance, ceinture de sécurité, code de la route, conduite accompagnée, délit de fuite, fourrière**

education **brevet, concours, DEUG, enseignement, équivalence, formation, licence, maîtrise, orientation, scolarisation, stage**. *See* school

electricity **certificat de conformité, EDF**

employment **contrat de travail, convention collective, durée déterminée, durée indéterminée, intermittent, publicité mensongère, temporaire, vacation**

employment agency **agence de placement, ANPE, temporaire**

endorse **endosser (un cheque)**

estate agency **agence immobilière, bail, dépôt de garantie, location,**

eviction **expulsion de domicile, loi Méhaignerie, maintien dans les lieux**

excise duty **accise, tarif, taxe**

executor (of a will) **exécuteur, testament**

factory inspector *see* work inspector

fax **fax, télécopie**

fees **barème, charges, dépens, frais, honoraires**
file **casier, fichier**
fine **amende, dédit, majoré, sanction administrative**
flat **caution, copropriété, gardien, location, pièce, quittance, standing, syndic d'immeuble.** *See* house-buying, tenant
form **bon, bulletin, certificat, copie, demande, expédition, feuille, fiche, formulaire**
franchise **concessionnaire, fonds de commerce, franchise**
fraudulent advertising **DGCCRF, dol, publicité mensongère**
funds **fonds.** *See* capital

GCSE **brevet.** *See* education, qualifications, school
grant **bourse, subvention.** *See* benefits
grievance **blâme, grief, préjudice**
guarantee **caution, dépôt de garantie, garantie, non-garantie**

handicapped people **allocation, assurance, carte d'invalidité, handicapé, invalide, mutilé de guerre, pension d'invalidité**
higher education *see* university
highway code **code de la route.** *See* driving
holiday **chèque-vacances, clôture, colonie de vacances, congé, fermeture, fête, jour férié.** *See* child-minding
hospital *see* clinic
hours at work *see* **convention collective, durée hebdomadaire du travail, durée quotidienne maximum du travail, heures supplémentaires, Inspection du Travail**
house-buying **acte de vente, assurance automatique acquéreur, compromis de vente, contrat de réservation, loi Scrivener, notaire, promesse de vente.** *See* flat

identity papers **carte de séjour, carte d'identité, livret de famille, relevé d'identité bancaire**
industrial tribunal **conciliation, Conseil de Prud'hommes, Inspection du Travail**
information office **agence de renseignements, syndicat d'initiative**
initials **lu et approuvé, parapher**
injunction **injonction**
inland revenue **fisc, impôt, perception, taxe**
insurance **assurance, mutualité**
invalid (1) **caduc, cour de cassation, irrégulier, nul**   (2) *see* handicapped people *and below*
invalidity benefit **allocation aux adultes handicapés, allocation aux mères de famille, allocation compensatrice de handicap, allocation d'éducation spécialisée, allocation des mineurs handicapés**

inventory **constat, huissier**

judge **juge, magistrat, tribunal**
jurisdiction **compétence, cour, juridiction, tribunal**
jury **jury**

Land Registry **matrice cadastrale**
law **arrêté, code, droit, loi, ordonnance**
lawsuit **action, affaire, contentieux, instance, justice, litige, procès**
lawyer *see* legal advice
lease **bail, fonds de commerce, franchise, sous-bail**
legal advice **avocat, avoué, conciliation, conseiller, Inspection du Travail, jurisconsulte, maison de l'avocat**
legal aid **aide judiciaire**
legally binding **acte, aide légale, contraignant, promesse.** *See* mandatory
libel **abusif, atteintes à la vie privée, dénonciation calomnieuse, parjure**
licence **autorisation, certificat, franchise, mandat, permis, pouvoir, procuration, redevance**
list of charges **chefs de la demande, registre du rôle**
litigation *see* court case
loan **aide personnalisée au logement, crédit, emprunt, hypothèque, prêt**
log-book **carte grise**
loss certificate **certificat de perte**

maiden name **nom de jeune fille**
maintenance **aliments, entretien, obligation alimentaire, pension.** *See* marriage
maintenance charges **charges**
majority **émancipation, majeur**
manager **direction, gérant, patron, syndic d'immeuble**
mandatory **facultatif, obligation**
marriage **communauté, concubinage, conseiller matrimonial, mariage, union libre.** *See* divorce, will
marriage agency **agence matrimoniale**
marriage certificate **acte de mariage, dispense de bans, livret de famille**
maternity allowance *see* child-minding
medical care **allocation, assurance maladie, bon de docteur, clinique, étiquette, feuille de soins, hôpital, vignette**
medical certificate **attestation médicale**
mortgage **emprunt-logement, hypothèque, prêt patronal**

name **nom, prénom**

national insurance **assurances sociales**. *See* deductions
no-claims bonus **bonus-malus**
notice (to do something) **préavis**

O-level *see* GCSE
offence **contravention, crime, délit, infraction, quasi-délit**
office **bureau, cabinet, caisse, direction, étude**
overtime **heures supplémentaires**. *See* hours at work

P45 **certificat de travail, licenciement, solde de tout compte**
paragraph **alinéa**
pass **autorisation, carte, licence**
penalty **astreinte, dédit, majoré**
pension *see* retirement
perjury *see* libel
permission **autorisation**. *See* licence, planning permission
planning permission **certificat d'urbanisme, coefficient d'occupation du sol, conformité, constructible, permis de construire, servitudes, viabilisé**. *See* below
plot **lot, lotissement, terrain**. *See above*
police **agent de police, commissariat de police, CRS, force publique, forces de l'ordre, garde champêtre, gendarme, hôtel, police, préfecture**
post office **boîte postale, courrier, envoi contre remboursement, lettre recommandée, mandat, minitel, postéclair, PTT**
postal order **chèque postal, mandat-lettre, mandat poste**
postpone *see* deferral
power of attorney *see* proxy
prescription **ordonnance**
privacy **atteintes à la vie privée**. *See* libel
proof of purchase **acte d'achat, acte d'acquisition, acte de vente, bordereau d'achat, reçu, souche**. *See* receipt
proof of receipt **accuser réception**
proof of sale *see* proof of purchase
property **bien, communauté, déclaration de ressources, foncier, propriétaire**. *See* seizure
proxy **autorisation, désigné, fondé de pouvoir, mandat, mandataire, pouvoir**
purchaser **acquéreur**

qualifications **certificat, équivalence**. *See* education, school

railcard *see* travel card
receipt **avis, quittance, récépissé, reçu, solde, souche, timbre-quittance**. *See* proof of purchase

Appendix of Sample Forms

1. Change of Civil Status

LA POSTE
CNE 210

CAISSE NATIONALE D'ÉPARGNE
☐ Livret
☐ Plan n°
☐ Compte

Nécessaire fait au BCL
Visa de l'Agent.

CHANGEMENT DANS LA SITUATION CIVILE

PC

titulaire (ancien état civil)

M., Mme, Mlle
en capitales nom patronymique
Prénoms
NOM d'alliance
NOM d'usage prénom du mari
ADRESSE (1)

Tél.

Code postal
(1) En cas de changement d'adresse, remplir le cadre « Nouvelle adresse ».

mariage

NOM du mari
en capitales nom patronymique prénom
NOM d'usage Date du mariage

Pièce présentée ☐ Livret de famille ☐ Fiche d'état civil
☐ Bulletin de mariage ou extrait de l'acte de mariage

Délivrée le à
Par

divorce

NOM de l'ex-mari
en capitales nom patronymique prénom
NOM d'usage Date du divorce

Pièce présentée ☐ Livret de famille ☐ Fiche d'état civil
☐ Expédition de l'acte d'état civil avec mention marginale du divorce

Délivrée le à
Par

nouvelle adresse

ADRESSE : Esc., Etg., Appt., etc.
(en capitales)
Résid., Bat., etc.
N° et nom
de la voie
Commune :

code postal bureau distributeur

IMPRIMERIE NATIONALE 7 118 048 O

183

émancipation

☐ Par mariage* célébré le _____

☐ Par déclaration du juge des tutelles de _____

en date du _____

Pièce présentée ☐ Livret de famille ☐ Fiche d'état civil

☐ Bulletin ou extrait de l'acte de mariage

☐ Certificat du greffe

Délivrée le _____ à _____

Par _____

* Pour une mineure remplir également le cadre mariage

erreur ou omission d'état civil

Erreur dans l'orthographe du nom

NOM _____
en capitales   nom patronymique

NOM d'alliance _____

NOM d'usage _____

Omission de prénoms ou inversion

Prénoms _____

Erreur dans l'indication de la date ou du lieu de naissance

Date de naissance _____ Lieu de naissance _____

Pièce présentée ☐ Carte nationale d'identité ☐ Livret militaire

☐ Livret de famille ☐ Fiche d'état civil

☐ Bulletin de naissance ou extrait de l'acte de naissance ou de mariage

Délivrée le _____ à _____

Par _____

autre cas — Nom d'usage

signature du titulaire

A _____ le _____
Signature

certification

Signature certifiée,
le receveur

Pièce d'identité

n° _____

délivrée à _____

le _____

par _____

T à D

2. Chemist's Form for Claiming Rebate on Medicine

cerfa
N° 60-3677

VOLET DE FACTURATION
DU PHARMACIEN OU DU FOURNISSEUR

RENSEIGNEMENTS CONCERNANT L'ASSURÉ(E) (1)

NUMÉRO D'IMMATRICULATION

NOM-Prénom
(suivi s'il y a lieu
du nom d'époux)

ADRESSE

CODE POSTAL

SITUATION DE L'ASSURÉ(E) A LA DATE DES SOINS

☐ ACTIVITÉ SALARIÉE ou arrêt de travail

☐ ACTIVITÉ NON SALARIÉE

☐ SANS EMPLOI ▶ Date de cessation d'activité :

☐ PENSIONNÉ(E)

☐ AUTRE CAS ▶ lequel :

RENSEIGNEMENTS CONCERNANT LE MALADE (1)

• S'agit-il d'un accident ?   ☐ OUI   ☐ NON   Date de cet accident :

• Si le malade est PENSIONNÉ DE GUERRE
et si les soins concernent l'affection pour laquelle il est pensionné, cocher cette case ☐

SI LE MALADE N'EST PAS L'ASSURÉ(E)

• NOM

• Prénom   Date de Naissance

• LIEN avec l'assuré(e) :   ☐ Conjoint   ☐ Enfant   ☐ Autre membre de la famille   ☐ Personne vivant maritalement avec l'assuré(e)

• Exerce-t-il habituellement une activité professionnelle
ou est-il titulaire d'une pension ?   ☐ OUI   ☐ NON

MODE DE REMBOURSEMENT (1)

☐ VIREMENT A UN COMPTE POSTAL, BANCAIRE OU DE CAISSE D'ÉPARGNE
Lors de la **première** demande de remboursement par virement à un compte postal, bancaire, ou de caisse d'épargne ou en cas de **changement de compte**, joindre le **relevé d'identité** correspondant.

☐ Autre mode de paiement

(1) **Mettre une croix dans la case de la réponse exacte**

J'atteste, sur l'honneur, l'exactitude des renseignements portés ci-dessus.

* LA LOI REND PASSIBLE D'AMENDE ET/OU D'EMPRISONNEMENT QUICONQUE SE REND COUPABLE DE FRAUDES OU DE FAUSSES DÉCLARATIONS (articles L 377-1 du Code de la Sécurité Sociale, L 441-1 du Code Pénal). *

Signature de l'assuré(e) ▶

• 3115 •

fabrègue s.a. saint-yrieix - limoges - paris

Appendix of Sample Forms

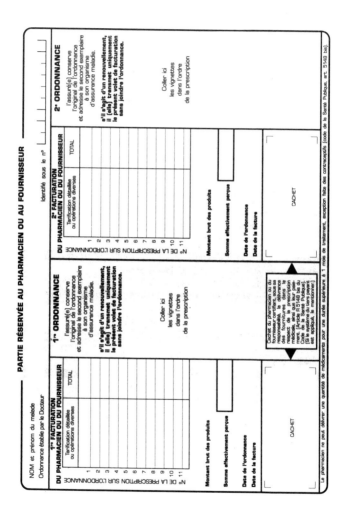

3. Lost Mail Form

LA POSTE ✈
CNE 33

Nécessaire fait au BCL

Visa de l'Agent

CAISSE NATIONALE D'ÉPARGNE

1er feuillet
à envoyer au Centre de CNE

☐ livret
☐ compte N° | | | | | | | | | | | | | |

⌐ ¬

DÉCLARATION DE PERTE

d'un livret ☐
d'une carte POSTEPARGNE ☐
d'un reçu CNE 21 ☐

└ PC ┘

titulaire

M., Mme, Mlle
en capitales *nom patronymique* _____

Prénom _____

NOM d'alliance _____

NOM d'usage _____ *prénom du mari* _____ Date de Naissance | | | | | |

ADRESSE _____

Code postal | | | | | | _____ Tél. _____

Bureau teneur du compte local : _____

déclarant s'il n'est pas le titulaire

M., Mme, Mlle
en capitales _____

ADRESSE _____

Code postal | | | | | | _____

Agissant en qualité de représentant légal ☐ mandataire ☐ autre ☐

perte du livret ou de la carte POSTEPARGNE

• S'agit-il d'un vol : oui ☐ non ☐ Heure de dépôt de la déclaration _____ h

• Si oui le récépissé de déclaration aux autorités de police est-il joint ? oui ☐ non ☐

Cas d'un livret

• Je demande l'ouverture d'un nouveau livret et m'engage à restituer l'ancien s'il est retrouvé

• Je désire retirer le nouveau livret au bureau de poste de _____

• Observations : _____

Cas d'une carte POSTEPARGNE

• Je désire le renouvellement de la carte : oui ☐ non ☐

• Je désire changer le n° de compte : oui ☐ non ☐

• Le code confidentiel a-t-il été divulgué ? oui ☐ non ☐

Montant du remboursement exceptionnel de dépannage éventuellement accordé au dépôt de la déclaration de Perte (opération non inscrite sur le livret) : _____

perte du reçu CNE 21

n° _____ délivré le _____ par le bureau de _____

signature du déposant

A _____ le _____ Signature du déposant :

réservé au bureau

⌐ **T à D** ¬

réservé au centre

Cas du livret

☐ Envoi du nouveau livret (en remplacement du livret signalé)

sous le n° | | | | | | | | | | | | | | |

Le chef de centre de CNE

⌐ **T à D** ⌐

└ centre ⌐

Cas de la carte

☐ Introduction du Code de blocage le | | | | | | | | à _____ h _____ mn

☐ La codification pour le remplacement automatique de la carte sous le

même numéro de code a été saisie le | | | | | | | *Visa de l'Agent*

☐ Suppression de la particularité P$_2$ — 1 le | | | | | | |

réservé au bureau

☐ Remis le livret n° | | | | | | | | | | | | | |

à M., Mme, Mlle _____

agissant en qualité de titulaire ☐   représentant légal ☐   mandataire ☐   autre ☐

A _____ le _____

Signature :

Pièce d'identité

⌐ **T à D** ⌐

_____ n° _____
délivrée à _____
le _____
par _____
Visa de l'agent :

└ bureau ⌐

AVIS AUX ÉPARGNANTS

Le vol ou la perte de votre livret, ou de votre carte de la caisse nationale d'épargne doit être signalé immédiatement au guichet d'un bureau de poste ou par téléphone au centre de caisse nationale d'épargne, et confirmé par écrit afin qu'une opposition soit enregistrée et que votre responsabilité soit dégagée en cas de malversation.

En cas de vol, une déclaration doit être déposée aux autorités de police. Le récépissé qui vous sera remis doit être envoyé soit au bureau de poste soit au centre de caisse nationale d'épargne qui gère votre compte, sous enveloppe non affranchie.

Si vous retrouvez votre livret ou votre carte vous devez le déposer obligatoirement au guichet d'un bureau de poste accompagné du présent duplicata.

réservé au bureau

_____

_____

_____   ⌐ **T à D** ⌐

_____

Visa de l'Agent

└ bureau ┘

4. Application Form for a Social Security Number

cerfa
N° 60-3833

SÉCURITÉ SOCIALE

VOLET 1
C.P.A.M.

DEMANDE D'IMMATRICULATION D'UN TRAVAILLEUR

(articles L 312-1, R 312-4, R 312-5, R 312-6 du Code de la Sécurité Sociale)

RÉSERVÉ C.P.A.M.

	C.P.A.M.	N° de document		CRAM	CEE

RÉGIME PRINCIPAL   Date d'effet

C.P.A.M. Prestataire   Centre de paiement

TRAVAILLEUR

IDENTITE ☐ Monsieur ☐ Madame ☐ Mademoiselle

Nom de naissance
(en majuscules d'imprimerie)

Prénoms
(dans l'ordre de l'état civil)

Nom d'époux
(en majuscules d'imprimerie)

Sexe ☐ Masculin ☐ Féminin   Nationalité : ☐ Française ☐ C.E.E.   ☐ Autre   Réservé CPAM

Date de naissance   Jour   Mois   An   Commune de naissance   *(pour Paris, Lyon et Marseille indiquer l'arrondissement)*   N° départ.   N° commune ou pays de naissance

RENSEIGNEMENTS PARTICULIERS

● *TRAVAILLEUR NÉ HORS DE FRANCE MÉTROPOLITAINE (qu'il s'agisse de personne de nationalité française ou étrangère)*

Pays de naissance du travailleur   Commune

Nom de naissance du père   1er Prénom

Nom de naissance de la mère   1er Prénom

● *RESSORTISSANT DE LA C.E.E. (application de la décision 117 de la C.E.E.)*

Préciser le numéro d'immatriculation dans le pays de nationalité

● *AUTRES TRAVAILLEURS DE NATIONALITÉ ÉTRANGÈRE (voir cas particuliers dans la notice explicative) :*

☐ Certificat de résidence N°   ☐ Carte de séjour N°   ☐ Carte de travail ou autoris. prov. de travail N°

ADRESSE

(éléments d'adresse complémentaires : villa, lieu-dit, lotissement, cité, résidence, bâtiment, escalier, étage)

N°   Voie
(R rue, BD boulevard, AV avenue, PL place, SQ square, CH chemin)

Commune

Code postal   Bureau distributeur
(à indiquer si elle est différente du bureau distributeur)

EMPLOI

● Date d'embauche   Jour   Mois   An   Lieu de travail

● Emploi du travailleur   N° d'immatriculation agricole (le cas échéant)

● Lien de parenté éventuel entre le salarié et l'employeur
(afin de déterminer le régime d'affiliation)

● Réservé aux employeurs occupant du personnel doté d'un statut de droit public : S'agit-il d'un agent titulaire ?   ☐ Oui   ☐ Non

EMPLOYEUR

IDENTITE   *(ne pas utiliser de cachet)*

N° SIRET   Code APE

Nom ou raison sociale

ADRESSE

(éléments d'adresse complémentaires : villa, lieu-dit, lotissement, cité, résidence, bâtiment, escalier, étage)

N°   Voie
(R rue, BD boulevard, AV avenue, PL place, SQ square, CH chemin)

Commune

Code postal   Bureau distributeur
(à indiquer si elle est différente du bureau distributeur)

Certifié exact à _____ , le _____   Signature :

La loi n° 78-17 du 6 janvier 1978 relative à l'informatique, aux fichiers et aux libertés s'applique aux réponses faites sur ce formulaire. Elle garantit un droit d'accès et de rectification pour les données concernant le travailleur auprès des organismes concernés.

S 1202 d
Cerfa 60/3833 11.90 CPAM 00.01202.1

Appendix of Sample Forms

SÉCURITÉ SOCIALE

VOLET 2
C.R.A.M.-INSEE

DEMANDE D'IMMATRICULATION D'UN TRAVAILLEUR
(articles L 312-1, R 312-4, R 312-5, R 312-6 du Code de la Sécurité Sociale)

RESERVE C.P.A.M.

C.P.A.M.	N° de document	CRAM	CEE

RÉGIME PRINCIPAL — Date d'effet

C.P.A.M. Prestataire — Centre de paiement

TRAVAILLEUR

IDENTITÉ — Monsieur — Madame — Mademoiselle

Nom de naissance

(en majuscules d'imprimerie)

Prénoms

(dans l'ordre de l'état civil)

Nom d'époux

(en majuscules d'imprimerie)

Sexe — Masculin — Féminin — Nationalité : Française — C.E.E. — Autre — Réservé CPAM

Date de naissance — Jour Mois An — Commune de naissance *(pour Paris, Lyon et Marseille indiquer l'arrondissement)* — N° départ. — N° commune ou pays de naissance

RENSEIGNEMENTS PARTICULIERS

● TRAVAILLEUR NÉ HORS DE FRANCE MÉTROPOLITAINE (qu'il s'agisse de personne de nationalité française ou étrangère)

Pays de naissance du travailleur — Commune

Nom de naissance du père — 1er Prénom

Nom de naissance de la mère — 1er Prénom

● RESSORTISSANT DE LA C.E.E. (application de la décision 117 de la C.E.E.)

Précise le numéro d'immatriculation dans le pays de nationalité

● AUTRES TRAVAILLEURS DE NATIONALITÉ ÉTRANGÈRE (voir cas particuliers dans la notice explicative) :
— Certificat de résidence N° — Carte de séjour N° — Carte de travail ou autoris. prov. de travail N°

REPONSE INSEE

N° d'inscription au répertoire + clé de contrôle

Jour de naissance

1re immatriculation

Observations

S 1202 d
Cerfa 60/3833 11.90 CPAM 00.01202.1

191

cerfa
N° 60-3833

SÉCURITÉ SOCIALE

VOLET 3
NOTIFICATION
D'IMMATRICULATION

DEMANDE D'IMMATRICULATION D'UN TRAVAILLEUR

(articles L 312-1, R 312-4, R 312-5, R 312-6 du Code de la Sécurité Sociale)

RÉSERVÉ C.P.A.M.

C.P.A.M.	N° de document		CRAM	CEE ☐

RÉGIME PRINCIPAL

Date d'effet

C.P.A.M. Prestataire

Centre de paiement

TRAVAILLEUR

IDENTITÉ

☐ Monsieur ☐ Madame ☐ Mademoiselle

Nom de naissance

(en majuscules d'imprimerie)

Prénoms

(dans l'ordre de l'état civil)

Nom d'époux

(en majuscules d'imprimerie)

Sexe ☐ Masculin ☐ Féminin   Nationalité : ☐ Française ☐ C.E.E.   ☐ Autre   Réservé CPAM

Date de naissance

Jour Mois An

Commune de naissance

(pour Paris, Lyon et Marseille indiquer l'arrondissement)

N° départ.   N° commune ou pays de naissance

RENSEIGNEMENTS PARTICULIERS

● *TRAVAILLEUR NÉ HORS DE FRANCE MÉTROPOLITAINE (qu'il s'agisse de personne de nationalité française ou étrangère)*

Pays de naissance du travailleur

Commune

Nom de naissance du père

1er Prénom

Nom de naissance de la mère

1er Prénom

● *RESSORTISSANT DE LA C.E.E. (application de la décision 117 de la C.E.E.)*

Préciser le numéro d'immatriculation dans le pays de nationalité

● *AUTRES TRAVAILLEURS DE NATIONALITÉ ÉTRANGÈRE (voir cas particuliers dans la notice explicative) :*

☐ Certificat de résidence N°   ☐ Carte de séjour N°   ☐ Carte de travail ou autoris. prov. de travail N°

ADRESSE

(éléments d'adresse complémentaires : villa, lieu-dit, lotissement, cité, résidence, bâtiment, escalier, étage)

N°   Voie

(R rue, BD boulevard, AV avenue, PL place, SQ square, CH chemin)

Commune

(à indiquer si elle est différente du bureau distributeur)

Code postal   Bureau distributeur

NOTIFICATION D'IMMATRICULATION

Nous, vous informons que le travailleur désigné ci-dessus, pour lequel vous avez fait une déclaration d'emploi,

☐ a déjà été immatriculé

☐ est immatriculé à compter du

Jour Mois An

Sous le numéro

Ce numéro est à rappeler dans toute correspondance

EMPLOYEUR

IDENTITÉ   *(ne pas utiliser de cachet)*

N° SIRET   Code APE

Nom ou raison sociale

ADRESSE

(éléments d'adresse complémentaires : villa, lieu-dit, lotissement, cité, résidence, bâtiment, escalier, étage)

N°   Voie

(R rue, BD boulevard, AV avenue, PL place, SQ square, CH chemin)

Commune

(à indiquer si elle est différente du bureau distributeur)

Code postal   Bureau distributeur

Certifié exact à _____ , le _____ Signature :

La loi n° 78-17 du 6 janvier 1978 relative à l'informatique, aux fichiers et aux libertés s'applique aux réponses faites sur ce formulaire. Elle garantit un droit d'accès et de rectification pour les données concernant le travailleur auprès des organismes concernés.

S 1202 d
Cerfa 60/3833 11.90 CPAM 00.01202

SÉCURITÉ SOCIALE

VOLET 4
A CONSERVER PAR
L'EMPLOYEUR

N° 60-3833

DEMANDE D'IMMATRICULATION D'UN TRAVAILLEUR

(articles L 312-1, R 312-4, R 312-5, R 312-6 du Code de la Sécurité Sociale)

RÉSERVÉ C.P.A.M.

C.P.A.M.	N° de document	CRAM	CEE

RÉGIME PRINCIPAL   Date d'effet

C.P.A.M. Prestataire   Centre de paiement

TRAVAILLEUR

IDENTITÉ   ☐ Monsieur   ☐ Madame   ☐ Mademoiselle

Nom de naissance
(en majuscules d'imprimerie)

Prénoms
(dans l'ordre de l'état civil)

Nom d'époux
(en majuscules d'imprimerie)

Sexe ☐ Masculin ☐ Féminin   Nationalité : ☐ Française ☐ C.E.E.   ☐ Autre   Réservé CPAM

Date de naissance   Jour Mois An   Commune de naissance
(pour Paris, Lyon et Marseille indiquer l'arrondissement)   N° départ.   N° commune ou pays de naissance

RENSEIGNEMENTS PARTICULIERS

● **TRAVAILLEUR NÉ HORS DE FRANCE MÉTROPOLITAINE** (qu'il s'agisse de personne de nationalité française ou étrangère)

Pays de naissance du travailleur   Commune

Nom de naissance du père   1er Prénom

Nom de naissance de la mère   1er Prénom

● **RESSORTISSANT DE LA C.E.E.** (application de la décision 117 de la C.E.E.)

Préciser le numéro d'immatriculation dans le pays de nationalité

● **AUTRES TRAVAILLEURS DE NATIONALITÉ ÉTRANGÈRE** (voir cas particuliers dans la notice explicative) :

☐ Certificat de résidence N°   ☐ Carte de séjour   N°   ☐ Carte de travail ou autoris. prov. de travail N°

ADRESSE

(éléments d'adresse complémentaires : villa, lieu-dit, lotissement, cité, résidence, bâtiment, escalier, étage)

N°   Voie
(R. rue, BD boulevard, AV avenue, PL place, SQ square, CH chemin)

Commune
(à indiquer si elle est différente du bureau distributeur)

Code postal   Bureau distributeur

EMPLOI

● Date d'embauche   Jour Mois An   Lieu de travail

● Emploi du travailleur   N° d'immatriculation agricole (le cas échéant)

● Lien de parenté éventuel entre le salarié et l'employeur
(afin de déterminer le régime d'affiliation)

● Réservé aux employeurs occupant du personnel doté d'un statut de droit public : S'agit-il d'un agent titulaire ?   ☐ Oui   ☐ Non

EMPLOYEUR

IDENTITÉ   *(ne pas utiliser de cachet)*

N° SIRET   Code APE

Nom ou raison sociale

ADRESSE

(éléments d'adresse complémentaires : villa, lieu-dit, lotissement, cité, résidence, bâtiment, escalier, étage)

N°   Voie
(R. rue, BD boulevard, AV avenue, PL place, SQ square, CH chemin)

Commune
(à indiquer si elle est différente du bureau distributeur)

Code postal   Bureau distributeur

Certifié exact à _____ , le _____ Signature :

La loi n° 78-17 du 6 janvier 1978 relative à l'informatique, aux fichiers et aux libertés s'applique aux réponses faites sur ce formulaire. Elle garantit un droit d'accès et de rectification pour les données concernant le travailleur auprès des organismes concernés.

S 1202 d
Cerfa 60/3833 11.90 CPAM 00.01202.1

SÉCURITÉ SOCIALE

DEMANDE D'IMMATRICULATION D'UN TRAVAILLEUR
notice explicative

Qui doit établir cette déclaration ?

En application des articles L 312-1, R 312-4, R 312-5, R 312-6 du Code de la Sécurité Sociale, L'EMPLOYEUR est tenu de déclarer **DANS LES 8 JOURS** qui suivent la date d'embauche, toute personne NON IMMATRICULÉE au régime général de la Sécurité Sociale, salariée ou travaillant à quelque titre ou en quelque lieu que ce soit pour le compte de celui-ci.

REMARQUE :

La présente déclaration doit être établie, chaque fois que le salarié n'est pas en mesure de présenter une carte d'immatriculation (ou une carte d'assuré social).

Où l'adresser ?

Cette déclaration doit être effectuée auprès de la caisse de résidence habituelle de la personne employée.

Comment doit-elle être établie ?

Les renseignements concernant l'état civil du travailleur doivent être rigoureusement conformes à un **DOCUMENT OFFICIEL D'IDENTITÉ**, par exemple :
- extrait d'acte de naissance,
- livret de famille,
- carte nationale d'identité,
- titre de séjour.

IMPORTANT :

L'IDENTIFICATION COMPLÈTE ET LISIBLE de chaque salarié, LE REMPLISSAGE CORRECT ET CLAIR de l'imprimé, évitent le risque, pour les salariés, d'être lésés dans leurs droits sociaux et pour les employeurs d'être importunés par des demandes de renseignements de l'administration.

Cas particuliers

● **Travailleur déjà immatriculé à la Sécurité Sociale**

Si celui-ci résidait précédemment dans la circonscription d'une autre caisse, il convient de l'inviter à faire une déclaration de changement de résidence auprès de son organisme d'assurance maladie.

● **Travailleur né hors de France métropolitaine.**

Dans ce cas, qu'il soit de nationalité française ou étrangère, joindre une pièce d'état civil ou sa photocopie, ou tout autre document officiel d'identité comportant, dans toute la mesure du possible, la filiation de l'intéressé. Pour les ressortissants marocains ou portugais, ce document sera obligatoirement un extrait d'acte de naissance.

● **Ressortissants de la Communauté Economique Européenne (C.E.E.)**

Les pays membres de la C.E.E. sont : l'Allemagne Fédérale, la Belgique, le Danemark, l'Espagne, la France, la Grèce, l'Irlande, l'Italie, le Luxembourg, les Pays-Bas, le Portugal, le Royaume-Uni. Leurs ressortissants ne sont pas soumis à une autorisation de travail à l'exception des ressortissants espagnols et portugais pour une période transitoire s'achevant au 1er janvier 1993. Ceux-ci doivent être titulaires jusqu'à cette date de

l'un des titres suivants : carte de résident, carte de résident privilégié, carte de ressortissant d'un Etat membre de la C.E.E. portant la mention "Toute activité professionnelle dans le cadre de la législation en vigueur", autorisation provisoire de travail.
Il est important pour les ressortissants de la C.E.E. de préciser sur l'imprimé leur nationalité.

● **Autres travailleurs de nationalité étrangère**

Il convient de vérifier, avant l'embauche, que le travailleur est autorisé à exercer une activité professionnelle salariée et lui demander de produire, selon sa nationalité, le titre de séjour ou (et) de travail dont il est titulaire pour l'exercice d'une profession salariée en France métropolitaine, principalement : carte de résident, carte de séjour temporaire portant la mention "salarié", certificat de résidence de ressortissant algérien (portant la mention "salarié" lorsque sa durée n'est pas supérieure à un an), autorisation provisoire de travail.

Pour tous renseignements complémentaires, adressez-vous à la préfecture, à la direction départementale du travail et de l'emploi (ou à l'inspection du travail).

Comment est constitué un numéro d'immatriculation ?

UN ASSURÉ SOCIAL EST CONNU PAR :

● son identité (nom de naissance, prénom, date et lieu de naissance)

(ET)

1	1 0	0 3	5 0	0 2 5	0 0 5	2 2
sexe	année	mois	départ.	commune	n° d'ordre	clé de contrôle
(2 : pour la femme)		de naissance		(attribué par l'INSEE)		

● son numéro d'immatriculation à la Sécurité Sociale.

Les volets 1, 2 et 3 doivent être envoyés à la caisse primaire d'assurance maladie du lieu de résidence habituelle du travailleur, l'employeur conserve le volet 4.

5. Application Form for a Post Office Bank Account

LA POSTE ➤
CNE 3 PE

CAISSE NATIONALE D'ÉPARGNE

n°

OUVERTURE DE COMPTE D'ÉPARGNE
sociétés, associations, etc...

A ☐
B ☐

versement _____ , ____ F

au profit de

Raison sociale _____
en capitales

N° Siret └─┴─┴─┴─┴─┴─┴─┴─┴─┴─┴─┴─┘

ADRESSE _____

_____ Tél. _____

Code postal └─┴─┴─┴─┴─┘

par

M., Mme, Mlle _____
en capitales

Prénom _____

ADRESSE _____

_____ Tél. _____

Code postal └─┴─┴─┴─┴─┘ _____

agissant en qualité de (1) _____

- déclare que la société, l'association, etc. n'est titulaire d'aucun livret A du même type ou un compte spécial sur livret du Crédit Mutuel ;
- désire que le compte d'épargne soit géré :

☐ sur livret

(2) ☐ sur relevés (compte POSTEPARGNE).

- Existe-t-il un compte chèque postal ? ☐ oui ☐ non (2)

Si oui son numéro └─┴─┴─┴─┴─┴─┴─┘ ☐ au centre de _____
(Joindre un relevé d'identité postal)

A _____ le _____

Signature de la ou des personnes habilitées

┌ PC ┐

└ ┘

┌ TàD ┐

└ ┘

(1) Président, directeur, trésorier, fondé de pouvoir, membre, mandataire
(2) Cocher la case utile

réservé au service

BUREAU

Dossier déposé au bureau de _____ Reçu CNE 21 n° _____

Sous le n° _____

avec CL ☐ 100 └────────┘ MONTANT

Mode de paiement
(autre que numéraire)

CHP ☐ 1 0 ☐ sans réserve

CHB ☐ 2

divers ☐ 3 9 ☐ avec réserve

sans CL ☐ 110

LIVRET EMIS : └─┴─┴─┴─┴─┘

au centre ☐ 0 Date de Valeur

CENTRE └─┴─┴─┘ PART └─┘ Naso └─┴─┴─┘ BURCL

Maximum autorisé _____

Nature du groupement _____

Si le maximum est plus élevé que celui des particuliers, le cas échéant,

Date de la décision _____

Pièces annexes _____

Fiche de renseignements 775 _____

_____

_____

_____

Imprimerie Nationale – 9 205010 O 39 F

Appendix of Sample Forms

1) Demande de compte d'épargne.

Les sociétés, associations, etc. régulièrement constituées, peuvent se faire ouvrir à la Caisse nationale d'épargne un livret A ou un ou plusieurs B[...] ci après le paragraphe 5 pour le cas particulier des organismes d'H L M et de crédit immobilier)

La demande de livret est signée par le délégué statutaire ou par un mandataire. Lorsque les statuts prévoient l'intervention de plusieurs personnes operations, la demande est signée conjointement par ces personnes

Le livret peut être remplacé par un compte POSTEPARGNE (les relevés de compte remplacent le livret)

2) Pièces justificatives.

Les pièces justificatives à fournir pour chaque société ou association, selon sa nature, pour ses rapports avec l'Administration étant variables pour les diverses operations faites par le groupement dans les bureaux de poste n'ont pas à être renouvelées à l'occasion d'un premier versement d'épargne si elles ont été fournies antérieurement. Toutefois ces pièces doivent être à nouveau produites a l'appui des demandes tendant à obtenir l'autorisation ministerielle necessaire dans certains c[...] pour porter l'avoir du groupement à un maximum plus élevé que celui autorisé pour les particuliers (voir ci dessous)

Si au contraire le groupement n'a pas encore fourni les justifications nécessaires, il y a lieu de proceder avant toute operation de versement à la constitution regulière du dossier

A cet effet, la société ou association doit produire

1. Un exemplaire ou extrait de son acte constitutif ou de ses statuts certifie exact et signé par le President ou le Directeur. En cas de production d'un extrait ci doit reproduire les dispositions indiquant l'objet, le mode de constitution et d'administration de la societe ainsi que le cas echeant, celles qui regissent la gestion des fonds.

2. Une piece variable selon la nature de la societe ou association, constatant que cette dernière est regulierement constituée et qu'elle a satisfait aux condit[...] de publicité prévues par la loi. Cette pièce est certifiée par le President ou le Directeur de la société de l'association.

3. Si les pièces specifiées aux paragraphes 1 et 2 ne designent pas l'administrateur delegue ou la personne chargée d'agir pour le compte de la societe et de donner quittance en son nom, il doit être fourni, en outre, des extraits certifiés conformes et legalises des deliberations des conseils, assemblées, comites, etc. qui ont procede à ces designations. Ces extraits porteront le specimen de la signature de la personne accreditee. Toutefois, ce specimen devra figurer sur la piece indiquee au paragraphe 1 lorsqu'il n'y aura pas lieu à production de la piece mentionnee au paragraphe 3

Les renseignements necessaires sont donnes à ce sujet par le receveur d'un bureau de poste quelconque (art. 85 du fascicule XV sur le service de la Caisse nationale d'épargne et annexe n° 9 du fascicule IX de l'Instruction générale sur le service des postes)

Les societes civiles, les societes cooperatives à caractere non commercial de consommation, de production, de construction, de credit, les societes ouvrieres d'ouvriers français, les societes d'assistance aux blessés des armees de terre et de mer les societes comprises sous la denomination generale de la « Croix-Rouge française », sont dispensees de la production de cette deuxieme piece

Les pieces susvisees sont transmises au receveur principal du departement ou se trouve le siege social du groupement, soit directement par les interesses, soit par l'intermediaire du receveur du bureau de poste

Pour les societes ou associations ayant leur siege à Paris, les justifications doivent parvenir, soit au receveur principal de Paris RP lorsque ce siege est situe d[...] un des arrondissements de Paris non pourvus d'un bureau central, soit au receveur du bureau central de l'arrondissement ou se trouve ledit siege

Avant de donner suite à l'acceptation du premier versement, le receveur des postes interesse doit avoir ete avise par le receveur principal, de la constitution dossier

3) Sociétés autorisées à effectuer de plein droit sur un livret A ou sur un compte POSTEPARGNE A des dépôts plus élevés que ceux des particuliers.

Peuvent, de plein droit, effectuer sur un livret A ou sur un compte POSTEPARGNE A des dépôts jusqu'à un maximum plus élevé que celui autorise pour particuliers, les organismes ci-après, régulièrement constitués

— sociétés mutualistes, unions et federations de societes mutualistes prévues aux titres 1er et II du livre 1er du code de la mutualite
— syndicats professionnels constitués conformement aux dispositions du titre 1er du livre III du code du travail
— sociétés ou caisses d'assurances mutuelles agricoles visées à l'article 1235 du code rural
— caisses locales et regionales de credit agricole mutuel regies par le livre V du code rural
— sociétés de credit maritime mutuel constituées suivant la loi du 4 decembre 1913 et les textes subsequents
— comités d'entreprises institués par l'ordonnance du 22 fevrier 1945,
— chambres d'offiers ministeriels
— comités ou sections de la Croix-Rouge française,
— sections du Touring club de France ou du Club alpin français,
— sociétés sportives,
— sociétés cooperatives de production,
— sociétés cooperatives de consommation
— sociétés savantes,
— sociétés de charite, orphelinats et asiles,
— sociétés d'assistance, de patronage et de protection, de sauvetage,
— sociétés philanthropiques,
— sociétés de secours formees entre les interesses avec ou sans le concours de tiers,
— sociétés de prevoyance,
— sociétés amicales d'anciens eleves,
— caisses de retraites,
— sociétés d'enseignement et d'education populaire,
— comités de patronage des ecoles,
— sociétés d'agriculture d'horticulture de sylviculture de viticulture de pisciculture,
— comices agricoles,
— sociétés musicales,
— sociétés nautiques,
— sociétés touristiques, syndicats d'initiative,
— sociétés colombophiles,
— associations de fonctionnaires,
— associations de propagande pour le rattachement à la cooperation ou à la bienfaisance, au même titre que les associations ou realisent les actes correspondants de cooperation ou de bienfaisance
— cercles, mess et foyers militaires s'ils presentent une organisation caracterisee de cooperation ou de bienfaisance
— clubs d'epargne à la condition qu'une disposition de leurs statuts les oblige à placer la totalite de leurs fonds disponibles dans une caisse d'epargne (sous reserve encaisse minime)
— paroisses catholiques ou communautes relevant d'autres confessions

4) Sociétés admises à effectuer sur un livret A ou sur un compte POSTEPARGNE des dépôts plus élevés que ceux des particuliers après autorisation spéciale.

Peuvent également être admises à effectuer sur un livret A ou sur un compte POSTEPARGNE des dépôts jusqu'à un maximum plus élevé que celui aut[...] pour les particuliers, mais seulement apres y avoir été autorisées par une decision ministerielle speciale, les societes ou associations ayant le caractere d'institutions mutualité de cooperation de bienfaisance ou de prevoyance (fasc. XV, art. 7.2)

La demande tendant à provoquer cette decision peut être faite en même temps que la demande de livret ou à une epoque ulterieure. Elle est redigée sur p[...] libre à l'adresse de Monsieur le Ministre des P.T.T., Direction des Services Financiers, Bureau D 1. Elle n'est pas expediee directement à cette adresse, mais remise au bu[...] de poste, appuyee d'une copie de la piece justifiant de l'existence legale de la société (ann. 9, fasc. VI de l'Instruction générale sur le service des postes) et d'un exempl[...] du d'un extrait des statuts. ces deux pièces sont certifiées par le president. Le dossier ainsi constitué est transmis par le receveur des postes au chef de centre de C[...] qui le fera parvenir à destination

Chacun des membres d'une société d'une association ou d'un groupement quel que soit, peut posseder un livret ou un compte POSTEPARGNE à son nom personnel, sans prejudice d[...] part dans le compte d'epargne collectif au nom de la société dont il fait partie

5) Sociétés autorisées à verser de plein droit sans limitation de somme.

Les organismes d'habitation à loyer modere et de credit immobilier sont autorises à effectuer des depots sur leur livret A ou sur leur compte POSTEPARGNE[...] sans limitation de somme

196